STUDIES IN MAJOR
LITERARY AUTHORS

Edited by
William E. Cain
Professor of English
Wellesley College

A ROUTLEDGE SERIES

STUDIES IN MAJOR LITERARY AUTHORS

WILLIAM E. CAIN, *General Editor*

Sports, Narrative, and Nation in the Fiction of F. Scott Fitzgerald

Jarom Lyle McDonald

Routledge
New York & London

813.52
F55 zm

Routledge
Taylor & Francis Group
270 Madison Avenue
New York, NY 10016

Routledge
Taylor & Francis Group
2 Park Square
Milton Park, Abingdon
Oxon OX14 4RN

© 2007 by Taylor & Francis Group, LLC
Routledge is an imprint of Taylor & Francis Group, an Informa business

Printed in the United States of America on acid-free paper
10 9 8 7 6 5 4 3 2 1

International Standard Book Number-10: 0-415-98133-6 (Hardcover)
International Standard Book Number-13: 978-0-415-98133-0 (Hardcover)

Library of Congress Cataloging-in-Publication Data

McDonald, Jarom Lyle, 1976-
    Sports, narrative, and nation in the fiction of F. Scott Fitzgerald / by Jarom Lyle McDonald.
        p. cm. -- (Studies in major literary authors)
    Includes bibliographical references and index.
    ISBN 0-415-98133-6
    1. Fitzgerald, F. Scott (Francis Scott), 1896-1940--Criticism and interpretation. 2. Fitzgerald, F. Scott (Francis Scott), 1896-1940--Political and social views. 3. Sports in literature. 4. Sports spectators. 5. Social status in literature. 6. Social classes in literature. 7. National characteristics, American, in literature. I. Title.

PS3511.I9Z6855 2007
813'.52--dc22   2006101160

Visit the Taylor & Francis Web site at
http://www.taylorandfrancis.com

and the Routledge Web site at
http://www.routledge.com

for Heather,
my inspiration,
always and forever

Contents

Introduction
Fitzgerald, Sport, and Social Interaction

Sport has, quite often, been a common motif in literature, functioning as theme, as setting, as allusion, and as metaphor. This is especially true in American Literature; as spectator sports moved to the forefront of American consciousness in the late nineteenth and early twentieth centuries, major and minor literary figures turned to sport as a way of comprehending some of the radical changes occurring in American life.

And while a variety of authors reacted to sport in a variety of ways, F. Scott Fitzgerald is unique among American authors in the approaches his literature took toward the significance of American sport. Fitzgerald is among the first of American authors to see sport as a *social* institution, one that went beyond functioning as an activity of leisure. In his perception, sport fit into larger concepts of social relationships, both relationships of immediate community as well as those of national identification. In doing so, sport had a noteworthy interaction with Fitzgerald's literary methodologies. As Fitzgerald used his literature to engage with history, nationhood, and the relationship between citizens of different class and/or status, his emphasis on social institutions provided a distinctive position from which to analyze the cultural context of spectator sports.

With this thesis in mind, let me emphasize that one cannot talk about the significance of F. Scott Fitzgerald's fiction without understanding the role that notions of social class and social status played in Fitzgerald's personal and literary life. Among other things, Fitzgerald treated his literary endeavors as a way to comprehend and understand better the class distinctions, class consciousness, and social mobility (or lack thereof) he saw in the modern American lifestyle. To interrogate issues of class and status, Fitzgerald would often focus on character types or conventions of setting and plot that served as microcosms of, or homologies for, much broader social systems. Much of his early literature consistently reworked motifs such as the poor young boy (or girl) losing the game of love to a wealthier counterpart or the talented artist hampered by economic and social constraints or boundaries. As he matured as a writer, Fitzgerald moved beyond simple character reworkings, recognizing deeper complexities and questions in such social situations and struggling to figure out how his questions about the ideologies of class related to ideologies of nationhood, race, religion, and gender. Everything became, for Fitzgerald, types of the social world: college and education, personal and family relationships, political happenings, the expatriate lifestyle, emerging media.

Yet while sport, in some ways, functioned similarly to some of these other institutions in terms of its relationship to social systems or its ability to be a target of Fitzgerald's social inspection, it also provided Fitzgerald a particular insight that these other social microcosms do not. Fitzgerald may not have found any actual answers to all his questions about social mobility that he seemed so earnestly in search of through his literature, but he returned to sports often in search of them. And as he sought to comprehend the system of social stratification in which he lived, spectator sports were an essential influence on his representation (or representations) of the American way of life. Moreover, his insights into the narratives associated with the institution of sport provide a center of examination that is invaluable for understanding the way other cultural institutions function in Fitzgerald's mind.

In this book, then, as I examine how Fitzgerald probed the roles of sport in American social formations, I will also read fictional narratives as responses to or conversations with some of the other narratives of sport. By doing so, I seek to investigate both the degrees of similarity and the differences between Fitzgerald's understanding of how sport works and that of other personalities of sport-related cultural rhetoric. I ultimately argue that Fitzgerald, through *This Side of Paradise, The Great Gatsby,* and his short stories, demonstrates how both sport (the rules, the history, the physical action) and stories told by and about sport worked together to structure concepts of social stratification. Fitzgerald's literary treatment of and influence by class-inflected sport culture reveal an often paradoxical phenomenon in both his own attitude to status-based power structures and in his analysis of the burgeoning American nationalism. He saw within spectator sport a consistent structure of stratification and hierarchy, even in the face of sport's own attempts to put forth the story that sport erases lines of difference and allows for egalitarian social relationships as a model of success—one built on individual talent rather than social ideologies.

As I put Fitzgerald's understanding of sport within the framework of social criticism, I make a distinction between the term "social class" and "social status." In my distinction, I find Max Weber's definitions of the two terms particularly helpful in understanding how class and status are separate but interrelated concepts. In "Class, Status, Power," Weber defines the term social "class" as a delineation of groups of power along purely economic lines. The term "status" becomes vital for Weber as he attempts to show that power structures are not inherently grounded in economic condition. For example, "Honor," such as that which comes through adulation of war or sport heroes, is a condition that can help create status. In fact, Weber theorizes that the power which comes from status is actually more important because it can lead to economic power, whereas the converse isn't necessarily true; economic accumulation does not always lead to status. For Weber, occupying a position of honor interacts with having command of economic resources, in that both states contribute to a more encompassing desire for power. "Man does not strive for power only in order to enrich himself economically," Weber writes, "[but] power, including economic power, may be valued for its own sake" (250). In Weberian terms, then, Fitzgerald, identifying relationships between sport and social formations, often focuses his attention more on concepts of status, especially in terms of the ways that sport leads to honor and the formation of status-groups. However, the word class itself does become important at different moments as well, especially in the ways that Fitzgerald sees sport connecting to national systems of class distinction. Throughout such investigations, Fitzgerald, too, sees "power" of privilege and elitism as the key concept to center on in the relationship between sport and status or sport and class.

The first chapter of the book, "'We Are a Very Special Country' : The Narrativization of Sport and the Fiction of a Classless Nation," will establish my argument in the framework of modern and contemporary American spectator-sport culture, a culture which finds its roots in concepts of emulation and vicarious participation. The major goal of chapter one is to situate the subsequent literary readings within an examination of the ways in which the institution of sport historically (and currently) perpetuates narratives of classlessness and equal opportunity while ironically reinforcing division along lines of social status—status that, while sometimes based in economic condition, is more often centered in celebrity adulation and emulation by spectators. Through analyzing common structures of contextual material, from autobiographies of star athletes of both early and late twentieth century to political anecdotes concerning the relationship between sport and status, I consider the pervasiveness of the following lines of reasoning: 1) As sport culture has become more of a fixture of celebrity in American culture, its focus on spectatorship has led to the narrativizing of sport—the idea that sport is perceived in terms of the stories that it tells and the myths that it disseminates; 2) Because of the physical nature of athletic competition, one of the most commonly disseminated narratives of sport centers around concepts of merit-based success; 3) This description of sport's inherent structures belies the actual reality that American culture has formulated (and continues to do so) its perception of sport through an emphasis on a spectatorship based not in meritocracy but in emulation and hero-worship, and thus the stories and myths that are most often disseminated actually reinforce the structures of social status rather than eliminate them; and 4) This conflict between the stories sport tells and the way sport functions is a significant homology for concepts of American nationalism, a nationalism taking pride in stories of egalitarian opportunity yet very often centered on the same hierarchical attitudes of meritocracy and exceptionalism seen in sport.

Once I lay out the theoretical groundwork of my argument, I begin to examine the ways in which Fitzgerald, himself so concerned with stories of hierarchy, status, and national attitudes, explores the paradoxes of sport society as a way to explore the paradoxes of American social life. Chapter Two, "Gridiron Paradise: Princetonian Football, American Class," will begin to read Fitzgerald by way of his first novel, emphasizing the historical convergence of American sport, American status, and American stories in his own narrative undertakings. Published in 1920, *This Side of Paradise* chronicles Fitzgerald's conception of the social relationships of the Ivy League community at Princeton. Fitzgerald considered Princeton in some ways a cultural microcosm for the nation, and often framed discussions of American culture as discussions of Princetonian culture. This is most striking in his investigation of college football at Princeton, a system which Fitzgerald once called "the most intense and dramatic spectacle since the Olympic games" ("Princeton" 94). I will investigate football at Princeton, both the historical Princeton which Fitzgerald attended as well as the fictional Princeton of *This Side of Paradise,* and deeply interrogate the rhetoric of the socially-inflected language through which Fitzgerald represents it. In doing so, I will show how Fitzgerald's first novel both passively allows as well as actively challenges dominant ideologies of social status formation. The novel, in which college football plays a quantitatively minor yet contextually crucial role, uses the settings, stories, and language of football specifically as a way to talk about spectatorship, emulation, and ideology, expressing both the possibilities and complications of trying to connect the stratified class system at Princeton with the act of living in a much larger and rapidly changing America.

Chapter Three, "'Idol of the Whole Body of Young Men': Football, Heroes, and the Performance of Social Status," will continue looking at college football but change genres, examining the role that football plays in the diverse corpus of short stories. Fitzgerald's stories dealing with football are extremely intriguing in their use of descriptive words such as "spectacle," "drama," and "play," words all with connections to performance. They also often contain strong correlative juxtapositions between the action of the game and theatrical settings, Hollywood personae, and a sense of audience-oriented, constructed rehearsing. As Fitzgerald narratively explores the connection between the game of football and some of these settings, such stories describe the physical action of football and its consequences not as an athletic competition but as a staged show, a play in which actors take on roles that bring them romantic and monetary accolades out of reach of the "spectators."

This observation is important for Fitzgerald as he more closely probes the ways that spectators "worship" football idols for their successful, skillful performances. Football for Fitzgerald is based in a social interaction of performance behavior that exists in the relationship between fan and spectator. Reading his football stories with this lens demonstrates the way in which he critiques the social status-groups that attempted to ground themselves in athletic success. Fitzgerald's football stories, in many ways, challenge their own literary heritage; rather than reincarnate well-known pulp sports figures such as cultural hero and American Dream icon Frank Merriwell, Fitzgerald's stories attempt to argue that the hero/idol figure's social tactics are, as strong as they might be, fantasy. Given such an assumption, Fitzgerald's short football stories argue that while football as a cultural narrative may have the power to allow for movement along a social hierarchy, such a phenomenon is not due to individual accomplishments or abilities but instead relies inherently upon the reactions of the crowd to a given performance. The performance of a football game thus sets the stage for a larger, social performance that creates the formation of status-groups around the idols and simultaneously recreates rituals of social relationship.

Chapter Four, "'Perfunctory Patriotism': Tom Buchanan, Meyer Wolfshiem, and America's Game," will move away from college football and look instead at baseball in the first part of the twentieth century. From the first significant use of the phrase "America's game," baseball has been continually labeled as the "national pastime" and the "game of the people," a sport structured to represent the best of American ideologies of egalitarianism and social equality. Yet while baseball did, in fact, gain rapid popularity in America because of certain structural characteristics that appealed to the emerging American middle-class, the application of ideals of an American character to baseball is largely based in a romanticism that ends up ignoring the real class tensions involved in such a spectator sport. Fitzgerald uses his masterpiece, *The Great Gatsby,* to see in this game a tension between mass

America, a group often labeled as the emerging middle class because of its increasing economic and social power, and the smaller groups of leisurely, upper-class sportsmen.

Though *The Great Gatsby* contains only a few scattered allusions to baseball amidst the complex collection of cultural objects, examining these episodes will demonstrate how Fitzgerald understands baseball as a key player in figuring out what people meant when they speak such words as "status" and "class." To restate, though the baseball allusions are few in number, they are crucial; the novel contains a textual history that is often overlooked yet which brings baseball to the forefront of discussion about Fitzgerald, sport, and class. A history of the revision process of the novel reveals a deleted passage from early galleys of *The Great Gatsby,* where the climactic moment in which Daisy, Gatsby, and Tom "have it out" occurs not in a private hotel room but instead following a long description of the group's outing to a Giants-Cubs baseball game. This textual history, both the initial inclusion of this anecdote as well as its eventual excision, will be read in terms of tensions of class and status.

In addition to the deleted passages, three specific textual passages existing in the final publication—James Gatz's childhood baseball schedule, Gatsby's Oxford-days cricket posing, and Meyer Wolfshiem's involvement in baseball—will demonstrate the degree to which baseball ultimately fails in its attempts to function as a rhetoric for the egalitarian "values" of the middle class. The use of baseball in the novel works together with the cultural context of baseball's early history (from the late nineteenth century through the first part of the 1920s) to make an argument for seeing baseball not as the national pastime, but as an ideological force which set the groundwork for the type of rhetorical recapitulations of the sports-based success myth that is at the heart of the contextual material which chapter one explores. Fitzgerald understands how the stories told about baseball, both individual narratives as well as cultural and historical ones, evolved into tools of American nationalism, specifically a middle-class nationalism with its own ideologies concerning the real and symbolic social significance of the game of baseball.

Ultimately, Fitzgerald's fiction helps us better see how spectator sports function as an ideological voice and are used by individuals to disseminate certain attitudes and beliefs about community, status, and nationhood. The union of a cultural analysis of sport culture and a literary analysis of Fitzgerald's fiction is also fruitful considering the way that society has permeated its participation of sport with a substantial emphasis on narrative structures. In other words, Fitzgerald understood the ways that culture "reads" sports, and his fiction often offers alternative or more complex "readings" that better comprehend the way that the stories of sport function in terms of influencing American class anxieties and debates over defining national identity. As I provide close, detailed readings of Fitzgerald's fiction in conjunction with associated historical records and cultural voices, I aim to investigate fully the understanding that the "peculiarly American" fiction of F. Scott Fitzgerald offers of the relationship between sport, spectator culture, and ideologies of social systems.

As a caveat, I must close this introduction by recognizing that paradoxes also inherently exist within Fitzgerald, an author seeking to investigate class structures in order to both criticize as well as embrace the hierarchical systems he so often encountered in American society. In his own attitude toward status-based power structures as well as toward burgeoning American nationalism at the turn of the century, Fitzgerald often found himself desiring simultaneously to be the privileged successor to the status bestowed through the "American Dream" narrative as well as to end the perpetuation of the myths which ultimately exclude all those who exist on the outside. As I investigate the ways in which Fitzgerald paradoxically responds to particular narratives of sport and ideologies of status, I demonstrate how Fitzgerald's conversations with American sport culture uncover the complicated ironies in American social stratification and reveal how the institution of sport culture historically and contemporarily perpetuates these same narratives, ideologies, and ironies.

Chapter One

"We Are a Very Special Country": The Narrativization of Sport and the Fiction of a Classless Nation

During the 1988 presidential campaign, George H.W. Bush stated, "I am not going to let that liberal Governor [Michael Dukakis] divide this nation. . . . I think that's for European democracies or something else. It isn't for the United States of America. We are not going to be divided by class" (qtd. in Kalra 1). Bush, of course, had a particular political agenda (relating to the upcoming election) in claiming that America desires to, or has the ability to, exist as a "classless" nation. But behind Bush's comments is an unacknowledged facet of his ideologies as well, one that speaks about the ways in which he sees the American nation in relationship to other nations around the world. Bush's statement exemplifies an idea that rests on a notion of American exceptionalism—the belief that America is, inherently, set apart from other nations.

Several months later, as Bush began his presidential term, he made his claims of how class should (or shouldn't) function in America the focal point of his inaugural remarks. In talking about America as a model for other countries, he stated,

> For the first time in this century, for the first time in perhaps all history, man does not have to invent a system by which to live. We don't have to talk late into the night about which form of government is better. . . . America today is a proud, free nation, decent and civil, a place we cannot help but love. We know in our hearts, not loudly and proudly, but as a simple fact, that this country has meaning beyond what we see . . . ("Inaugural Address")

The ideas expressed behind phrases of this nation's "better" government and "simple fact[s]" of America serving as an standard are, of course, not unique to Bush by any means. On the contrary, Bush's speech taps into one of the most common sentiments of the motif of American exceptionalism, that America, as a nation, is "better" because its form of government is based in supposed democratic ideals, ideals that somehow create the type of classless social system that Bush called for during the election debate.

Apparently when it came to speeches, George Bush saw much value in espousing notions of American exceptionalism, as he only three weeks later elaborated upon such ideas in yet another public address. In this particular oration, Bush stated,

> The main ingredient in each person's success is individual initiative. It always has been, and it always will be. So I would say, if you're willing to work hard and make sacrifices, you can accomplish just about anything you set your mind to. And that's what the American dream is all about. ("Congratulations to 49ers")

Bush's goal here appears to be making a connection between the collective "successes" of the American nation and the manner in which that success could be attributed to the work of its individual citizens. The phrase "American Dream," a phrase which many consider trite and worn out in both sociological and literary studies, has nevertheless persisted in being one of the most pervasive ideas espoused by American citizens, emerging in all forms of discourse and across all institutions. Politically speaking, rarely is an individual elected without overtly espousing a belief in American exceptionalism and in the ability of the "American Dream" to raise citizens to the top of the social and economic ladder. It is no wonder that George Bush made such concepts an integral part of his campaign and of his subsequent presidency.

The story of a nation giving all individuals equal access to the accumulation of wealth, status, and success is a powerful narrative, one which, by relying on words such as "opportunity" and "mobility," encourages convictions of the primacy of internal qualities over external; the American dream sees hard work and dedication as factors for both social and monetary success and dismisses theories that suggest environment, genealogy, and history could shape one's social status or class position. American society has ideologically embedded the American Dream motif into culture to such a degree that a large portion of citizens wholeheartedly believe Bush when he states that classes don't exist in this nation. In fact, as Paul Fussell notes in *Class: A Guide Through the American Class System,* the concept of class has consistently been "remained

murky. And always touchy. You can outrage people today simply by mentioning social class" (1). To so many American citizens, America is the singular
nation that has a history (and, they would claim, a future) free from division
and stratification.

Ironically, though, Bush's campaign statements, according to Paul
Kalra, are incongruous with his own position within the American social
system; Kalra notes that a claim of a classless nation, coming from the lips
of a "tennis-playing, fly-fishing, quail-hunting, Skull and Bones Yalie [who]
is by all accounts . . . a millionaire many times over on his own but also
the son of a U.S. Senator and married into money" is proof that, despite
Bush's protests, social stratification undeniably *does* exist in America (2). This
reaction in part centers its rhetoric on issues of economics, pointing out the
inherent contradiction in an Ivy-League educated man of wealth, position,
and connection trying to make a case for America as a land free from social
stratification. In fact Kalra's choice of critical language is even more intriguing than his overall argument; the words through which Kalra frames his
response leads into a discussion of privileged economic status by categorizing
Bush according to a series of his favorite sporting pastimes. Thus Bush is not
just a Yale alumnus, he is not just a millionaire, but he is a "tennis-playing,
fly-fishing, quail-hunting" millionaire. Bush's privilege is couched as much
in what sports he engages in as in where he went to school, what his father
does, or who he is married to. Moreover, as the first activities which Kalra
mentions, these labels of sporting activity are prominently displayed as the
epitome when it comes to describing Bush's social status through his activity;
the image of Bush-as-sportsman is that which serves as the idiomatic entry-
way to the other images of privilege and elitism.

That a social analysis turns to sport to find images with which to make
an ideological comment is not surprising, by any means. As Michael Oriard
notes, "The rhetoric of sport and play . . . reveals American attitudes towards
many things—business, politics, religion, personal relations—not directly
related to sport and play" (xi). In *Sports Talk: A Dictionary of Sports Metaphors,*
Robert Palmatier and Harold Ray compiled over 1700 distinct usages of sporting images and language within discourses of other cultural institutions. Using
sports to talk about other parts of culture is so commonplace, one needs only
turn on talk radio or read the local paper to find language, images, and metaphors of sport. In fact, the last in the series of quotes from George Bush at the
beginning of the chapter, in which he mentioned the term "American Dream,"
was part of his address congratulating the San Francisco 49ers on their Super
Bowl win; Bush was, at that time, specifically attempting to draw a comparison between success on the football field and success in other areas of life.

Yet while this is certainly a poignant insight into one of the functions of sport in American society, there is more going on in Kalra's critique of George Bush's campaign declarations. In Bush's case, he is not just the victim of a clever pundit using a sporting metaphor as another way of labeling him "upper class"; that is, Kalra does not merely use sport as a rhetorical displacement for a discussion of more "weighty" class issues. In this particular instance, the three sporting events aren't even metaphors at all, but an actual list of some of Bush's favorite pastimes. George Bush plays tennis, fly fishes, and hunts quail, and in fact was often photographed and written about while spending time engaging in such sporting endeavors.

And while Bush also participated in watching or playing other sporting events as well (he, like his son, is an avid baseball fan, for example), in this particular instance he is specifically *not* described in terms of such other sports. Kalra's response to his claim that America "will not be divided by class" wouldn't have the same effect if he had called him a "baseball-loving Skull and Bones Yalie." The reason Bush is labeled by these particular sports is because of their embodiment of the irony in his invocation of the American Dream motif. While claiming that each citizen has an equal opportunity for advancement, Bush ignores the fact that his choice of sporting activities are accessible to him yet inaccessible to others. And while Bush's economic class is certainly a factor, his advantages when it comes to the sports he can play are also a function of his social position—that is, a result of the power which his elite status grants him. As Jay Coakley notes:

> People with resources are able to organize their own games and physical activities in exclusive clubs or in settings inaccessible to others. When this happens, sport becomes a tool for elite groups to call attention to social and economic differences between people and to preserve their power and influence in the process. (qtd. in Sugden 311)

Money might be an important factor in determining social position, and birth and family might be likewise important, but rhetorically sport, in the attitude of Kalra's language and analysis, is a framing discourse of Bush's privileges and the subsequent "class" with which he is associated. Despite his rhetorical protests, when Bush is figured as the "sportsman" and done so specifically in reference to sports such as tennis or hunting for quail, sport becomes a substantial symbol of his own privileged standing. And consequently, Bush's social standing thus becomes a signifier of a class-stratified nation.

Such is the argument of this entire book, that sport, as an American institution, often attempts to embody narratives of equal opportunity for social mobility; yet more often than not, sport actually ends up revealing and, in some cases, reinforcing the divided social composition of the American nation. Sport belies the inherent disconnect in American class development and formation of American notions of status, perpetuating the narrative of the "American Dream" while simultaneously suppressing its possible fulfillment.

Specifically, there are two unique factors of sport that allow me to make this assertion about American sport and social stratification. The first such element is the overt spectator culture that first developed around sport in the late nineteenth and early twentieth centuries. As John Bale writes, "whether at local, regional or national level, sport is, after war, probably the principal means of collective identification in modern life. It provides one of the few occasions when large, complex, impersonal and functionally bonded units can unite as a whole" (qtd. in Cronin 51). The cultural activities of the American sports scene—those of gathering at the ballparks, reading or listening to emerging media, worshipping sports heroes—cultivate a community of spectatorship that, if not conscientiously engaged with, perpetuate myths that certain people earn privilege, status, and even wealth through taking advantage of the same opportunities which have supposedly been accorded to all citizens by virtue of their "Americanness."

The second factor is the tendency to see sports in terms of stories. The records of sporting activity in America are found across many disciplines and in many textual objects: histories, personal accounts, popular culture periodicals, sportswriting, radio and television broadcasts, images, and so forth. But a unifying theme running through each of these objects is the focus on narrative. Sport has become narrativized, in that it is seen less as a historical occurrence and more as a reconstruction of events through an adherence to supposed conventions of storytelling such as plot, character, and theme. According to Hayden White, this is an inevitable process. He writes that when looking back on past occurrences (which, he would argue, is the only way we can examine history—by looking back on it), events "must be not only registered within the chronological framework of their original occurrence but narrated as well, that is to say, revealed as possessing a structure, an ordering of meaning, that they do not possess as a mere sequence" (5). In other words, the act of narrativization is one that, by necessity, imposes an artificial structure upon events and seeks to situate events within a larger paradigm of belief.

In applying White's theories of narrativization to sport culture, then, it becomes clear that the act of recognizing the ways in which society narrativizes sport works together with the act of understanding better the emergence of a spectator culture surrounding sport. This claim relies upon the following reasoning: because sport spectatorship places emphasis on events sustained over a period of time, it naturally gravitates toward a sense of history. This, then, leads to the narrativization of sport. Because spectators continue to have a propensity for seeing sports in terms of stories, spectatorship thus becomes an activity not just of watching the action of a given game but of re-telling the stories that they find there—or more accurately, that they create there. Spectators must invest their energies not in any sense of reality, but in history and mythology. Of course, such a statement then encourages an extremely significant question—exactly what sorts of stories does spectator culture find through the act of narrativization? The short answer is that the most common recurring narrative in spectator sports is either one of the tensions between communal acceptance and privileged exclusion or one of the supposed successes of a talent based solely in individual success. Because of this, spectator culture is thus inextricably linked to issues of social division. The long answer requires a deeper look into spectator sport culture.

SPORT AND SPECTATORS

As I am laying out the rationale underlying my look at the way that society narrativizes sport by propagating myths of the American Dream, I need to mark out the bounds of my methodology. In doing so, it would be useful at this time to explain what assumptions I am accepting when I talk about spectator sports. In the introduction, I dealt with the differences in defining the word "class" and the word "status," seeing Max Weber's distinctions as vital for understanding how sport leads to the accumulation of status. Several other words are just as important to demarcate. The term "spectator," finding its roots in a concept of visual perception, is very literally defined as one who watches, in this case, a sport. Centering a discussion of sport on the act of watching and observing also reveals a linguistic relationship of paramount importance between the word "spectator" and the word "spectacle." Spectacle, a word associated most prominently with theatre, is a concept often attributed initially to Aristotle. As Aristotle defines drama in his *Poetics* he refers to spectacle as one of the main components of drama, albeit the least important in his eyes. Aristotle's understanding of what constituted spectacle—for him spectacle referred to any of the visual elements of drama such as costume or sceneography—evolved into the common usage of the term; a spectacle today is generally an activity or event noteworthy for its emphasis on the visual, even to excess. Theatre is thus still considered very much grounded in spectacle, as is as film. But in addition to this more denotative use, the term is, contemporarily, often applied to both current and historical occurrences where events take on a "spectacular" nature not just because of the emphasis on things visual but also because of the involvement of a great deal of emotion from a great number of people. Political rallies, family reunions, news conferences, museums, all become "spectacle" in the sense that they attract large bodies of observers who interact with each other as they are "spectating" the events at hand.

This assumption, that spectacle is based in notions of collective emotional involvement, is significant for defining spectator sports. In an article aptly entitled "'Buzzer Beaters' and 'Barn Burners,'" Jennings Bryant and Steven Rockwell argue that the spectacle of sport is enjoyable precisely because it elicits sensations of excitement, suspense, and aggression (326–7). Such a claim relies on the fact that spectator sports are not just watched by individuals, but by mass crowd, presumably all experiencing similar emotions. As sporting crowds gather together to watch a given contest, the actions of the crowd can be seen as a form of participation. Yet the type of participation encouraged by spectator sports is not one of playing, but instead one of "fanship"—a unique form of interaction that includes acts of cheering, of wearing team colors and jerseys, and of following a team's successes or failures from game to game. Such activities are all methods of identification that give spectators an avenue for *vicarious* participation, placing themselves in the role of team member rather than mere observer, and thus changing what we mean when we talk about the spectator in spectator sport. Michael Real and Robert Mechikoff write that "the nature of the interpretive community in which the sport fan places himself or herself and the degree of psychological identification with the athletes contributes to dimensions of both breadth and depth in fan mythic identification" (324). The spectacle in spectator sports, then, is when a game is played before such a mass of people, gathering for a presumably united purpose and engaged in simultaneous forms of fanship (ones reliant upon some form of identification), and, in an observation that will be significant later in this analysis, often drawn from a homogenous population. Sport spectacle is less about who resides and what takes place on the field, and more about who resides and what takes place *around* the field. As a spectacle observed by a community of fans, a particular sporting event is transformed from a mere game to a vibrant social activity, one significant in its reliance upon the spectators observing the action of the athletes.

Let me use college football as an example that both historicizes as well as exemplifies my discussion of the new "spectatorial culture."[1] As football evolved into the American form of the game from other sports such as rugby and soccer, it was not unusual for people to gather together to watch the games as a crowd. Yet generally speaking, in the early days of football these crowds did so in smaller numbers, in sporadic patterns, and often without specific purpose other than curiosity or passive leisure. However, as the nineteenth century progressed, the scale of attendance grew, the consistency and repetition of attendance grew, and bodies formed that gave structure to a more spectatorial nature of the game. While initially groups of friends used to get together to watch other friends play (and vice versa), soon club teams were formed on college campuses that became more popular than the informal, make-shift teams. It wasn't long before quite a few students were attending some of the informal matches between Yale-Princeton or Harvard-McGill, and eventually an 1876 conference set up by two Princeton students fixed a system for colleges to have official teams. The conference also created an organizational body and system of competition that would, in an organized, consistent manner, allow teams from different colleges to compete against each other year after year.

This transfer of association allowed for football to serve as a snapshot of the universities' performances; football became a public face of a given university. School rivalries evolved, and promoting a football team was a way for a given university to claim superiority by virtue of a cultural synecdoche; if one school's team beat another in football, then by extension the school itself must be better. In this way, football allowed students and alumni of a given university to find a greater investment in the success of the football team, which in turn gave them more reason to attend the game and participate as a fan and began to create lines of hierarchy within universities and between them. Records of the first college football game, between Rutgers and Princeton in 1869, tells of Rutgers fans all wearing scarlet bandanas on their heads and the Princeton fans uniting in chorused cheers such as "Tiger sis-boom-ah Princeton!" (Bernstein 7), cheers which drew verbal lines of connection between the team's identity and the University's identity. The *Atlantic Monthly* reported that by 1890 "the athletic spirit in the colleges is greatly stimulated by the fact that the whole college feels a personal interest in the [football] players" (65). John Higham writes that "a rage for competitive athletics and for outdoor activities of all kinds was sweeping the campuses of the nation. A combative team spirit became virtually synonymous with college spirit; and athletic prowess became a major determinant of institutional status" (78). With such a desire for unity with the players on the football team, with a desire for emulation, spectators were the motivating force behind the emergence of phenomena such as school colors. Soon to follow were team nicknames and mascots, all furthering the visual show. By the turn of the century, football had ceased being a game; it was a spectacle represented through, to use a Walter Camp description from an 1891

Harvard-Yale game, a mass "waving madly to and fro in the brilliant sun-shine" ("College" 386). The spectacle of football was centered in the crowd and one that created a unique relationship between player and fan.

In defining spectator sports, this phenomenon of the growth of fanship at college football games is representative of the socialization of sport. The most significant point of my definition is that spectator sports encourage a sense of community from the fans gathered together to observe the spec-tacle; they construct a crowd that attempts to act together as a mass body. This notion of community is a virtual one, foregrounded in the act of seeing something simultaneously. The concept of identification is extended from being part of the crowd to being a part of the team, the bodies in the stands becoming an extension of the bodies on the field. Thus fans can feel a sense of membership and unity that develops into the lifestyle of following sports, from year to year, rather than just watching them in periodic fashion. And most often, a fan's identification with a given team is both a creator and a function of community. Spectatorship becomes a routine, one that dic-tates behavior and (in some cases) even agency. Moreover, because spectator sports encourage people to identify with players and fellow fans, and to do so through codified, ritualistic patterns of attendance, cheering, and so forth, such sports encourage interaction between fans outside the bounds of the actual spectacle; in other words, even when the games are over common fan-ship becomes a way to structure social relationships.

It might be tempting to assume that fans generally tend to associate with other fans with whom they can relate or with whom they find superfi-cial commonalities (geography, age, career, etc); historically, of course, this is related to the collegiate nature of a sport such as football or the phenomenon of industry-based baseball teams, where people associated with those with whom they already associated with. But spectatorship also tends to work the other way, reinforcing homogeneity along the lines of more intangible char-acteristics such as behavior and ideology. Such identification between fans while they are also trying to identify with a team is based in much more than occupation or alma mater. Economic background and nationality, the two fundamental concepts of Bush's tirade about class in America, are as much a part of inter-fan identification as geography.

This is not to assume that only spectator sports enjoy the type of sta-tus-based connection that lies at the center of analysis in this argument. As is evident with the quotations from George Bush and the responses they elicited, often the choice itself to participate in "non-spectator" sports has significant social implications. Nor is it my claim that only members of a certain status or associated with a particular class participate (as player or, more often, as fan) in spectator sports while others shun them. Indeed, some would claim that in the contemporary sport scene, tennis—a traditionally "upper-class" sport, is also a spectator sport (although, undoubtedly the type of tennis that Bush engages in would not be played before thousands of cheering fans but instead at a club or private court). What is important in figuring a connection between sport and social standing is that sport participation is directly related to structures of class formation. To use specific examples, in the case of football in the nineteenth century, both players and fans were drawn from the upper-middle and upper classes, as they were the ones with the principal economic means for attending the prestigious universities where organized competitive football grew to prominence and were also those invested in the status-based ideologies of the Ivy leagues. But at the same time that college football was clearly an upper-class pursuit, a sport such as boxing demonstrates the complexities in trying to correlate specific sports with a specific class on a one-to-one basis. Some analyses consider early boxing a spectator sport of the working class, where champion boxers became heroes for certain groups of people who identified with each other along racial, national, and ethnic lines as well as ones of economic background and social position. Novelist James Michener, in his tract *Sports in America*, quipped, "With a little practice, one could look at the Boston newspapers of any given era, and by seeing who was fighting whom, determine where the various immigrant groups were on the social ladder" (211). Though Michener was speaking of the athletes, the activity he describes could, theoretically, ascertain assumptions about the social standing of those cheering a given boxer at a given time. Yet John Higham sees early boxing as a middle or even upper-class pursuit, placing it within his larger framework of progressive activism which was fundamentally respectful to rules and restrictions of culture (79). Such an argument points to a historical competition like "Gentleman Jim" Corbett's defeat of Jack Sullivan in 1892 as the beginning of scientific, technical boxing that appeals to middle-class mind sets of progress and professionalism as well as upper-class notions of taste; boxing would thus be a paradoxical form of "genteel violence." My point is that rather than try to neatly categorize specific sports along social lines, people of any class find sociality in sport. Sport participation itself is a social activity, and this inextricable connection is what leads to understanding better sport's narrativization.

Having somewhat defined spectator and spectacle, I recognize the importance of also, on some level, dealing with the definitional issues of the word "sport." Christian Messenger does a good job of defining the term as it differs from other words often thought to be synonymous; his definition distinguishes sport from games of play, games of leisure, and games of fortune. According to Messenger, game is an overarching category, one that relies upon "any form of playful competition whose outcome is determined by physical skill, strategy, or chance" (4). In this rubric, formulating a definition of sport would thus focus on identifying types of games in which physical skill is the primary function. With such a definition, a game such as chess would not be a sport, because chess places a majority of the emphasis on strategy and very little on physical competition. Gambling, with such an emphasis on luck, would also not be a sport, despite some strategy needed and even, in some cases, physical performance. Messenger's definition is significant in what it claims about sport, that physical ability is of foremost importance, trumping intellectual ability and factors beyond the control of an individual player. In fact, with such an athlete-centered definition of sport, culture is even more inclined to perpetuate the narrative of an ability-based system of distinction and forget about social environment—defining sport in such a way inextricably connects it to the physical capabilities of an individual body while simultaneously ignoring anything having to do with the spectators that form the majority of the society of sport.

But in talking about sports themselves, I am interested not as much with what actual activities constitute a "sport" but more so with the cultures created by playing, watching, reading about, or talking about sports. To define the word "sport" in some sense requires a recognition of these cultures, a task that I accomplish by delineating it according to a linguistic classification of sorts. This task is best accomplished circumlocutiously, by defining two other words. The first of these is "institution"; I employ this word much as Cheryl Herr does, as "any collective creator of discourse that tends to repeat its messages and to shape social behavior through that repetition" (4). Such a definition employs the second key term, "discourse," roughly defined as the means, inextricably linked to historical moments, of specifying knowledge. The "institution" of sport, then, would be the collective creative voices of sport—we might think of these voices as those of the athletes (including their practice and behavior), those of the spectators/fans, and those of the sportswriters. I would also include their media in talking about the institution of sport—sports writing (newspaper and periodical), sportscasting, sport literature, and so forth. The "discourse" of sport would be the assumptions, arguments, and conclusions put forth by the various institutional objects within their specific textual records; discourses are, by nature, rhetorical, and discourses perpetuate certain ideologies, whether they are dominant or marginalized.

And finally, in addition to breaking down "sport" according to its voices and rhetorics, it is also useful to do so by classifying different functionalities of what is bound up in the term; I do so by thinking of the "structures" and the "narratives" of sport. As I use it, "structure" refers to how sport works: the rules, the histories, the physical action, the relationship between athlete and fan, the organizations, etc. A "narrative" of sport focuses on my extended discussion of narrativization earlier, looking away from the games themselves and instead at the stories and the telling of stories, whether these be stories of individuals, teams, specific sports, specific sporting events, sporting myths, and the like.

SPORT AND STORIES

Working with the above definitions of particular terms, especially that of "narrative" of sport, let me briefly go into more depth in analyzing the inherent narrative structure that sport lends itself to. Doing so will subsequently allow me to locate some of the most pervasive stories of sport that emerge, how these stories create a cultural context, and, later on, how that context is expressed in terms class and social status, both contemporarily and historically. When I make the claim that people seek to see sports in terms of stories—meaning plot, character, detailed action, and so forth—I find strong connections between such an occurrence and the phenomenon of celebrity. The "cult of celebrity," a term often used to describe the way that society "worships" the personae put forth by individuals whether those personae are accurate or not, has existed in America for centuries, making icons out of figures from politics to entertainment. Daniel Boorstin, in *The Image: A Guide to Pseudo Events in America,* defines celebrity as a person who is known simply for being well-known (46–48). His argument is that celebrity is self-perpetuating and has a basis more in visual images of itself than in anything tangible. Boorstin also describes a concept of the "pseudo-event," an event staged merely to further the function of celebrity in society. Boorstin's ideas relate to some of the work of Max Horkheimer and Theodor Adorno, who, for example, discuss the idea of "the culture industry"—a focus on objects, institutions, and entertainment events designed specifically for consumption. Entertainment of the culture industry is easily reproducible, easily disposable, and very much wedded to a notion of spectacle. In combining Boorstin's theory of pseudo-events with the Frankfort School's concept of the culture industry, celebrity becomes a sort of phenomenon that perpetuates itself by demanding public surveillance of celebrities' private lives merely for more spectacle (in effect, making people famous for being famous), creating an elaborate mixture of narrative and consumption. Media such as newspapers, radio, film, television, and now the Internet capture images of celebrity and situate them firmly in the public sphere; using the images of celebrity figures as a way to appeal the demands of the community of admirers of a particular icon.

The cult of celebrity thus aids in the formation of status groups, creating a complex relationship between fan and idol (one that I deal more in-depth with in Chapter Three. At this point, the facet of the cult of celebrity that is most significant for my investigation is the way in which, in this constant deluge of images that creates and reinforces celebrity status, the community of fans is not merely satisfied with visual representations of celebrities but seek after the stories *behind* the images. Timothy Dugdale argues for the role that celebrity biography plays in the relationship between fan, idol, and culture of celebrity. He asserts that biographies, whether formal, published books or informal reports and captions that accompany various pictorial accounts of celebrities, serve as "social texts," creating a form of cultural history surrounding the subjects of the narratives in which spectating and speculating go hand in hand (2). Generally speaking, society is interested in actual details about the private lives of very public figures such as Hollywood stars and candidates for political office to reassure the public that such figures are, in fact, not the "larger-than-life" personae that they might seem on screen or in print.

Most celebrities face a society that is engaged in a continual search for the "stories" of what these idols are doing on a particular night in a particular place, "stories" of their relationships, and often "stories" of the mistakes they make. Richard Schickel claims that this incessant drive for the narratives of celebrity is also a form of identification. "We know them, or think we do," he writes. "To a greater or lesser degree, we have internalized them, unconsciously made them a part of our consciousness, just as if they were, in fact, friends" (4). This internalization of the minute details of a celebrity's life creates an illusion that the fan knows the celebrity on a deeply personal level because of the level of detail involved in the retelling of certain anecdotes that are, for most people, kept private. For Schickel, the cult of celebrity thus bases its strength in the star figures becoming "intimate strangers" to the community of adoring fans. Of course, in some ways this point of analysis is ironic in that when fans treat celebrities as close friends, they create the fantasy of getting closer to their idols but at the same time create a level of worship that places the celebrities even higher upon a social pedestal. The objects of worship are made the center of a social circle and accorded status and honor which paradoxically separates them even further from the spectators.

When it comes to the story-seeking of the sports fan, there are subtle differences that make the narratives of sport apart unique in American society's incessant search for celebrity detail. It is true that athletes are quite obviously (and historically have always been) subject to a similar sort of celebrity adulation, and certain sports stars, especially in recent years, face the same type of visual, public revelations of their personal and private lives that have often been associated with politics, Hollywood, and rock stars. Yet the institution of sport creates a second type of celebrity narrative that is still just as powerful, if not more so, in producing the type of identificatory relationship between spectators and their heroes. These secondary narratives of sport are found in the "storylines" that people, often those involved in media, create around a given sporting match-up, throughout a particular sport season, or across a sport star's career. These stories do not have as their goal merely a snapshot report of a real person's day-to-day private life; they are not designed to be privileged, private information about public figures. Instead they are narratives of the institutions and structures of sport, in effect creating a "celebrity" status for the sport itself. Moreover, they are based firmly in the spectatorial nature of sport, in that they are stories created and disseminated by masses of fans. Figuring sport as celebrity draws lines of homology between the narratives connected to individual athletes and the narratives of sport connected to particular games, statistical records, or the like. This serves to compound both the illusory closeness and the status-based worship that begins with treating the sporting figures as celebrity.

Seeing sport itself in terms of principles of celebrity also eschews the fleeting pleasure of most forms of celebrity that attempt to be ultra-contemporary and fail to develop any real lasting memory. Instead of solely focusing on the latest tabloid headline, stories of sport inextricably ground themselves in history. The meta-narratives that order sport are forms of myth, myths that use history and commonalities with other cultural myths as a way of finding order in the happenings of "celebrity" events that, in actuality, have a sense of randomness about them. In other words, by seeing sports in terms of stories, fans try to get closer to sport by creating an illusory sense of control over events that are completely out of control, at least from the point of view of the spectator.

A contemporary example will help demonstrate the way that viewing sport as story-based uses history and myth as a way for spectators to, through developing a fantasy of control and also engaging in ritual acts of worship, harness the "celebrity" of an entire sports team, in this case the Chicago Cubs. In the fall of 2003, the Cubs were in the playoffs of Major League Baseball, and needed to win one more game in order to advance to the World Series. The Cubs were the "feel good" story of the year, not having been to a World Series since 1945 and not having won one since 1918. Their playoff run was a national phenomenon, being covered in evening newscasts and newspapers all over the country; the Cubs' story was the hot watercooler conversation and their players had quickly become household names.

Playing on their home field in this particular game against the Florida Marlins, the Cubs had a 3–0 lead with one out in the eighth inning of the game—in other words, they only needed to make five more outs to "make history" and make the entire country (outside of Miami) ecstatic. Mark Prior, the Cubs' star pitcher, seemed to be cruising through the game with ease, making few if any mistakes, and showed no visible signs of tiring. By all indications, the Cubs seemed poised to finish it off and move on to the World Series. With Florida player Luis Castillo at bat and a man at first, the fans at Wrigley Field were cheering, yelling, and screaming, certain that the team they had come to support would win—truly a mass of people acting as one. When Castillo hit a weak fly ball that started drifting foul, everything seemed normal.

Then Steve Bartman—a fan whose name has since become the butt of too many jokes to count—reached out to try to catch the fly ball, a common occurrence at a baseball park. At the same time, the Cubs left fielder, Moises Alou, jumped and reached his glove over the wall to try to catch the foul ball and make the second out of the inning. Alou's arm was brushed, either by this fan or others sitting near him (fans who have, in the minds of other spectators, all been collapsed into the single image), and the ball bounced away, leaving the batter Castillo with another chance. In the dugout, Marlins player Mike Redmond reportedly then turned to Derrek Lee and, knowing of the celebraic "well-knowness" that the Cubs had, ironically remarked, "Let's make *that* kid famous." Following this, the next seven players all reached base, and the Marlins suddenly had an 8–3 lead. They went on to win the game, the next game as well, and the Cubs were eliminated from the playoffs.

As ESPN baseball analyst Jayson Stark wrote,

> We all know in sports that things happen that can't possibly happen. . . . But how do we explain *this?* How do we explain what happened in Wrigley Field on a Tuesday night when the Cubs were five outs away from the World Series—and wound up in a twilight zone of despair and disbelief? ("Say it ain't So")

For the next several weeks, sports talk radio personalities debated this very question, "How do we explain this?" The answer that might be the most accurate response would be another question, one that wonders what purpose there might be in seeking for an explanation to the events. After all, the very nature of sport denies the ability to predict the future based on what has happened; there was no way to know what would happen in a given game, and hence no real way to explain what did happen. But when things seem to be predictably turning out one way, and then radically change, those who feel invested in the game, those who occupy the position of "spectator," try to find a way to structure what they've witnessed; they try to find meaning in that which seems random.

Fans of the Chicago Cubs turned away from the facts of the game at hand and instead towards the narratives of history in search of explanations. This wasn't the first tragic ending for a Cubs season; several others throughout the twentieth century have been amply chronicled. In 1945, the last time the Cubs were playing in the World Series, a Chicago tavern owner, Billy Sianis, tried to bring a pet billy goat to the first game and was rebuked. Apparently, at that time Sianis muttered, "Cubs, they not gonna win anymore." The Cubs lost the game and eventually the entire series. In 1969 they were nine games ahead of the New York Mets in their division as the season was coming to a close, when during a particular game a black cat came onto the field and circled Cubs third baseman Ron Santo. The Cubs faded down the stretch, and the Mets (who were given the nickname "The Amazin's" after that season) took the championship and eventually the World Series. In 1984 they were, as they would be in 2003, a single game away from winning the pennant when the Cubs first baseman, Leon Durham, let a ball roll through his legs. The Cubs lost again, lost the next game, and sat home while the San Diego Padres played in the World Series. As fans in 2003 turned to this string of historical events, they saw the seemingly inexplicable happenings of this October as the continuation of a pattern, a chain that had begun in 1945 and was dictating the outcome of contemporary games. In doing so, Cubs fans also latched onto a particular story that had arisen in each of those historical seasons, a story that Sianis, owner of the billy goat, had placed a literal curse on the Cubs that they could not escape. In other words, they saw in the 2003 playoffs a continuation of the curse narrative, the next logical step in the story that had begun in 1945. The 2003 playoff loss was viewed as inevitable, almost natural, given the storyline that fans constructed by viewing their tragic history through an eye of narrativization. As Stark quipped, "Just when you think they've run out of tragic scripts for their never-ending archives, they even top themselves" ("Say it Ain't So"). As the story goes, the Cubs will always be cursed, Cub players will always be cursed, and Cub fans will always be cursed. But at least the fans know this is the case.

In turning to history, not just the actual details of history but the myths which had grown up around such events, the 2003 game they had witnessed would no longer exist as a random act of confusion but would instead be a part of a valid, continued plot—not the plot that they had hoped for, but a coherent narrative nonetheless. Following this loss, Rob Neyer of ESPN wrote,

> most of us can predict with a great degree of certainty what we'll be doing tomorrow and the next day and the day after that. One thing we *don't* know, however, is who's going to win the next game. Yet, in retrospect it seems as if the Cubs were somehow fated to lose. ("Why Do We Care so Much?")

Such uncertainty can create enormous anxiety in fans that take so much time and utilize so much energy investing themselves in identification with the teams they are supporting. Questions that seem easy to answer at one point are left unanswered. But throw in a nearly 60-year-old story about a goat, and suddenly it all makes sense. Eric Dunning sees this as a vital component of sport, specifically connecting the security that one finds in being able to predict a sport narrative to the security that one desires within a social community: "Under such conditions, social life becomes more secure, more regular and more calculable" (48). Because narratives are inherently plot-driven, and plots have identifiable components and logical progression, they allow spectators to structure reality in a coherent, consistent, and most importantly predictable manner.

Along these same lines, as fans participate in the narrativization of sport, they very often engage in ritualistic activity in conjunction with the stories they tell. Chicago Cubs fans have adopted behaviors bordering on worship—not just of the players they adore, but of the legends and mythologies associated with their team. The story of the curse has become as much a part of being a Cubs fan as the more typical acts usually associated with fanship. Cub fans inaugurate each season with performative rituals of parading billy goats around the stadium and re-enacting the story of Sianis in 1945. As much as Steve Bartman became a pariah in Chicago for his participation in the latest instantiation of the curse narrative, he has also become an image for new forms of fan identification with the team, from fans dressing like he was dressed that night to a local Chicago restaurant blowing up the ball at the center of controversy and serving it to their customers to eat. Such ritual, symbolic behaviors are not ways to bestow status upon Bartman or Sianis, but upon the entire team; the spectators, the community, intensify the social interaction through the act of narrativization.

This is a significant factor in sports' appeal in modern culture. Because of the participatory nature of spectator sports, fans are accustomed to seeking more ways of identification with the team or the player they are supporting.

If fans are going to enact certain practices that will, in their eyes, link them to their idols, then they would naturally desire a certain degree of control. The fan-player relationship is the foundation of the community that the spectacle of sports creates, and those contributing as spectators only continue to participate if they feel they can have control. So, by viewing sports in terms of controlling narratives, and ritualistically engaging with those narratives, spectators acquire a more tangible method of participation. They are no longer just bystanders, but are active players themselves because of their ability to use the stories to predict what will happen. More importantly, finding the storylines in sport creates a bridge between the often disparate factors in the internal and external life of a fan. Commonalities between sporting events and the lives of the spectators are lines of identification that are even more powerful than common geography, school affiliation, and so forth. If a sport has a particular storyline, or if a particular athlete has an easy-to-identify and easy-to-retell story behind his success, spectators can identify events in their own lives that have those types of storylines and the narratives become powerful links that create the illusion of a closer relationship between spectator and fan. The narrativization of sport, whether it is of a particular game, a particular season, or a particular player's athletic career, creates a shared heritage within the constructed community of the sporting spectacle. Sport thus also becomes a way for structuring other aspects of life, ultimately leading to the numerous metaphors, allusions, and rhetoric of sport that find their way into other cultural institutions as we saw in the first anecdote of this chapter about George Bush.

SPORT AND STATUS

As the act of creating stories out of sport immerses sport in notions of celebrity, ritual, and communal interaction, the narrativization that extends beyond individual players ironically returns to bind up individuals more complexly in ideologies of status. In fact, because sport lends itself to the formation of powerful, social-structuring narratives (as witnessed through the story of the Cubs Billy Goat Curse), it would make sense that the most powerful narrative in American social life, that of the "American Dream" and its relationship to status formation and subsequent class division, would be a prominent thematic element in the narrativization of sport. In Elliot Gorn's words, sport has become "a sort of idealized version of the American social structure, offering equality of opportunity purely on the basis of merit" (4). Despite a lack of solid, empirical basis, sport fans often perceive that the various players or teams of a given sport start in a position devoid of status—on a "level playing field," so to speak. Spectator sports create a sort of fantasy which postulates that each competitor possesses similar opportunities and similar environmental advantages. Thus, spectator culture often assumes that success in athletics is due to qualities of virtuous endurance and greater natural-born talent. Given this assumption, as spectators vicariously participate in sport by finding stories in the ways described earlier, they consistently focus, whether consciously or not, on couching these narratives within language representative of the American Dream narrative. Doing so also draws grand analogies between the success of an athlete within a sporting community, the success of a citizen within a social community, and the success of a nation within a global community. In other words, because the competitive, physical nature of athletic contests result in a winner and a loser, the fans for whom these spectacles are staged thus assume that the winner deserves to be there, and is "exceptional" in his/her relationship to other members of the given community. This cultural logic asserts that such a player or team is an embodiment of the "common American citizen" who uses physical talent, physical ability, and physical hard work to reposition him/herself socially, the social mobility leading in some cases to economic improvement but in all cases to an increase in esteem, honor, and status among those occupying the position of "spectator."

For example, take a ubiquitous sport hero of the early twentieth century: Red Grange, who played college football for the University of Illinois and later professionally for the Chicago Bears. Grange was, with the exception perhaps of Babe Ruth, the preeminent name in spectator sports during the 1920s. The facts surrounding his success on the gridiron are prolifically documented; he accumulated over 3,600 yards running and 31 touchdowns in only 3 years of college, and proportional statistics during his nine-year professional career. Yet his status as an icon of early twentieth century sport is attributable not to his respectable statistics, which have long since been eclipsed, but instead to a particular narrative, that of Grange's "success story." The narrative of his life, as it has evolved through various textual representations, attempts to portray Grange as the figure of a common American athlete who is able to embody ideals of opportunity and individualism on his road to football greatness. Such a story sees his athletic success as a way of talking about his social success and, eventually, as a metaphor for national success.

If Dugdale's argument about the role that biography plays in the formation of celebrity is valid, then it is logical that an autobiography would serve as a specialized, testimonial form of Dugdale's "social text." Therefore in discussing the mechanisms of the narrative of Red Grange, turning to Grange's autobiography can shed light upon the way that the narrative of his sporting career reveals the connection between sport, story, social status, and national ideals. As Grange himself tells it, he spent his early life in the small hamlets surrounding the lumber camp where his father worked in Pennsylvania. The first pages of his autobiography detail the landscape of his surroundings: "a picturesque setting of giant hemlock trees, clear, cool creeks, green grass and majestic mountains" (3). By beginning the story of his life with an image of a virginal landscape, unscathed by "the nearest railroad" or "the closest towns," Grange paints his upbringing as one of pristine newness, still preserving the appearance of the landscape of the American continent when the nation was in its infancy. Grange's landscape description is ideological; he connects himself to a concept of American innocence and metaphorically posits his early life as a new beginning. In doing so, he is setting himself apart from his heritage and severing himself from a notion of historical genealogy. This ahistorical conception of a body is a fundamental tenet of the American Dream motif as well as of the belief of American exceptionalism. As those cultural narratives purport, the American nation, as an undiscovered country, was unfettered by histories of social stratification and was subsequently able to assume its destiny as the superior nation based in new forms of ideological governing and social relations. Writing with his sporting career behind him, Grange's underlying comparison here thus makes the argument that just as America supposedly broke free from European social structures in order to spring forth with an untainted system of living, the story of his athletic success began in a similar fashion. His future football success is thus here implicitly compared with American national success.

Football prominence and national exceptionalism are also, in this way, both situated within the discourse of social class. In addition to espousing ideological beliefs by way of his landscape description, Grange also tells his story as one of humble economic beginnings. Reminiscing on his move to Wheaton, Illinois, during elementary school, Grange states that "I realized more and more the advantages of growing up in Wheaton. Had the family remained in Forksville, I might have ended up as another Huckleberry Finn" (7). Grange moves from figuring the self as a new nation to figuring the self as a "common boy," to the degree that Huckleberry Finn represents such a notion. The metaphor here allows Grange to universalize his story in the sense that it is no longer just the narrative of an individual, but one of a shared literary heritage. It also centers his story on social class by virtue of his statement that he escaped becoming Huckleberry Finn. Huck Finn, a character excluded from society by both internal and external forces, would represent the low end of the national social system. The Huck Finn invocation also creates a reverse metaphor, perhaps forming a Grange-as-Tom Sawyer model, still endowing

Grange with a notion of "common" upbringing and economic status but also allowing him to paint himself as one taken in by society and allowed to participate in the story of individual American success.

Following this initial literary comparison, Grange's next paragraph makes the connection between this statement of social status and his involvement in sport. He writes, "I hated school just like any other kid and was resigned to it simply as a duty. The more important part of living came after school when I was able to play football, basketball, and baseball with my pals" (7). In other words, he started off like Huckleberry Finn and would have continued to see his life play out according to those narrative lines, but his move to Wheaton and his escape from Huck's fate is metaphorically centered in terms of the specific advantage of playing sports with his friends. Sport becomes an agent of change; Grange tells his story in such a way as to position sport as the fundamental instrument of mobility in his life. He persists in emphasizing that he found himself low on the ladder of class, noting that "none of us had uniforms, but improvised by cutting off the pant legs of our oldest trousers and added padding where needed most" (7). But as he continues to narrate his life, his physical talent and ability in sport (especially football) literally moves him along and provides him with all those things that Huckleberry Finn was excluded from, and throughout the autobiography Grange isn't shy about sharing what these advantages are. Football allows him to get an education; football becomes his career; football gives him the chance to star in Hollywood movies.

In his most poignant moment of casting his life as an incarnation of sport-as-American Dream, Grange relates an anecdote surrounding his signing a professional contract. As he retells the conversation between him and his agent during their first meeting, Grange underscores the sense of economic mobility which football provided for him. According to Grange, when he first met with Charlie Pyle, then owner of several Illinois movie houses, Pyle greeted him by saying, "'How would you like to make one hundred thousand dollars, or maybe even a million?'" (91). For the reader of the book, then, in less than one hundred pages Grange has moved from a character of American innocence to a prospective millionaire, a mammoth social ascent resulting, according to the logic of this particular plot, completely from his ability to play football. In fact, as he concludes his autobiography, Grange overtly sermonizes his story in terms of what his athleticism and his hard work have allowed him to perform:

> Through football I've been able to meet and get to know many thousands of wonderful people. . . . Football has enabled me to do and see most of the things I wanted in life and made it possible to earn a

good living through the years. . . . when I was a kid the only thing I thought about was athletics. It was my whole life and I put everything I had into it. The future took care of itself. When the breaks came I was ready for them. Any boy can realize his dreams if he's willing to work and make sacrifices along the way. (177–78)

Grange couches his story in language of dreams, work, and sacrifice, the common tropes of an "American" rise to the top and the supposed qualities of a typically American character as put forth by the narratives of exceptionalism. Ironically, while his conclusion universalizes the narrative, transforming his story into the story of "any boy," Grange specifically tells his tale in terms of what football enabled *him* to do. When taken in light of his earlier comparison between himself and the birth of the innocent nation, Grange, when speaking of "any boy," implicitly includes in his meaning only American boys—or perhaps more appropriately, American boys who are like him. Grange's is a story "universally" applicable to only a very particular group, a nation of youth who, like Grange, might identify themselves as trying to escape their own Huckleberry Finn-like fates and who would fall in line in considering Grange an effective model of success. Grange's autobiography ultimately makes two paradoxical arguments: 1) that individuals actually have this capability, that all have the chance to equal his athletic and subsequent social success, and 2) that sports, at least those in which an individual is "willing to work and make sacrifices," is an enabling power for those able to be like Grange.

This use of the tropes of achieving social dreams as a way to connect the stories of sport to those of social mobility is hardly unique to Red Grange's rhetoric in his autobiography. If anything, such cultural logic has become more copious as time has progressed. Today, an athlete is almost at a disadvantage (in terms of the chance of becoming an adored sporting celebrity) if he or she cannot tell a story (or does not have a story told about him/herself) in terms of the hard work necessary to succeed or of the ways in which physical performance can overcome environment or unfair circumstance in order to achieve iconic, celebrity status. And often, such language is invoked as a way to speak about athletes who have been marginalized in ways other than economic as well, fusing a particular person's social status and economic standing with his or her racial identity or gender under the concept of "disadvantages that needed to be overcome." A sampling of American sports icons demonstrates the degree to which the narrative pattern of seeking after a uniquely American form of achievement is so inculcated with the making of a star. For example, culture sees Hispanic baseball players such as Roberto Clemente or Sammy Sosa as ones who not only used baseball to better themselves economically, but also used the game as a literal tool of mobility, allowing them to immigrate to the United States. The image of immigration is the quintessential motif of the "American Dream" story.

Such a motif also reinforces ideologies of America as a superior, "promised land" nation. Stories of Clemente always emphasize him growing up in Puerto Rico and working on a sugar cane plantation. Narratives of Sosa's life always depict him living in the Dominican Republic, shining shoes and supposedly playing baseball with a glove made from a milk carton. Factually, of course, these histories may or may not be grounded in kernels of truth. However, in terms of narrativization, it makes no difference. History now tells these stories as a triumph over such humble conditions, made possible through athletic talent and individual hard work. Because baseball was the "work" in which Clemente or Sosa was involved, these narrativized histories figure their immigration as a physical success which inevitably leads not only to an escape from the financial conditions in which they were born, but to an American stardom, giving them the chance to change their national affiliation along with their economic status. In fact, the images behind these stories also implicitly tell a tale of overcoming racial conditions; working on a plantation or shining shoes are as much references to historical African-American motifs of slavery or the Jim Crow period as they are to Central American economic practices. In this way, America uses the stories of Clemente and Sosa to see baseball as a racial emancipator at the same time it is functioning as a social or a national one.

More examples of this layering of the social power of sport with other factors of identity include Billie Jean King, who, as the rhetoric often goes, realized the "American Dream" through her hard work and perseverance, pioneering the movement toward better gender equality in sport by beating Bobby Riggs; Jackie Robinson, who, according to the historical narratives, fulfilled the "American Dream" by single-handedly ending segregation in professional baseball; and Jesse Owens, who, in an oft-repeated tale of his early life, was born poor and sickly in Alabama, but pushed past his environment and developed his great speed through his dedication to the manual labor jobs he often took to help pay his family's bills.[2] Casual retellings of Owens's athletic accomplishments also focus on his race, noting the significance of winning four gold medals at the 1936 Berlin Olympic games amidst countless insults, threats, and slurs from Adolph Hitler and the rampant Aryan sentiment in Berlin at the time.

Owens's story is particularly interesting in relation to examining the tenuous yet culturally ubiquitous conception that rises out of the narratives of the "American Dream," the notion that that sport exemplifies America as a nation of superior opportunity as well as success. As is the case with Sosa and Clemente, Owens's economic conditions are palimpsestically linked to his racial identity; however, his position as Olympic athlete places him even more prominently in a more visible celebrity role, the role of national hero. Stories of Owens's Olympic success create an ideological axis that runs from individual class and race, to questions of community and status, to collective nationalism. Lincoln Allison notes the pervasiveness of the emphasis on national identification through the Olympic venue, arguing that the games belie their supposed international flavor and instead perpetuate exclusionary nationalism through uniforms, national symbols, and medal tables (346). In Owens's case, specifically, by winning four medals and being placed on a podium with the United States' national anthem playing and the American flag being raised, he is literally converted into a metonymy for the nation itself, a cultural phenomenon that then allows for the narrative juxtaposition of his story with the story of the nation. Owens's individual endeavors are glossed over, as are even his racial ones, as his accomplishments are appropriated by an ideology of American patriotism. He loses his own identity and is no longer a successful Olympic athlete, but instead becomes a trope. The metonymy operates through narrativization, continually retelling a story of a figure that, by virtue of his well-publicized successes, represents a nation that can overcome depravation *and* racism *and* fight the spread of Nazism. Owens the individual is transformed into Owens the icon, a symbol of how to live the American life. His is a story of race that is subsumed by his story of class, which in turn is subsumed by the supposed ideals of American spirit and the story of American exceptionalism which make an idol out of Owens. Ironically, rather than eliminating hierarchy, the cultural formations of Owens's story actually reinforces hierarchies—in this case, hierarchies symbolized in treating Owens as a figure of national status.

The transformation of narratives that are at their root stories of economic condition, or of lowly positions of status, into ideologies of American nationalism continues in contemporary society. Thousands of inner-city youth today play basketball in the streets as a way of participating in their own version of the "American Dream"; according to the rhetoric, basketball is their only chance of going to college, or, given the recent success of Kobe Bryant, Kevin Garnett, and Lebron James, foregoing education altogether while still reaping millions of dollars in NBA stardom and endorsement deals. Such economic advancement through sport is desirable not just for the accumulation of wealth or commodity, but for the accumulation of celebrity; the masses of aspiring basketball players are seeking to be basketball *stars,* celebrities no longer lost in the masses but settled in the position of idol. The same scene is repeated in Central American countries, where youth view baseball as literally the only way for economic advancement, for social change, for international stardom, and for immigration to the United States (an action which, for them, just reinforces the first three). It is still an "American" aspiration to such individuals, as baseball supposedly expands the borders of access and redefines the America that is being talked about.

Interestingly enough, it is precisely the spectatorial nature of sport that perpetuates the hold that the American Dream narrative has on these youth. Because athletic stars develop a form of celebrity, and because there is such a cultural desire to see sports in terms of narrative, youth who watch these stars play, hear the stories, and then engage in sporting activities themselves do so with the hope of mimicking the results that they have witnessed. Spectatorship, as a form of emulation, vicarious participation, and identification, leads to actual participation and emulation. And the more the stories are retold, the stronger this illusion becomes. Professional baseball recognizes this, and has established baseball "academies" in countries such as the Dominican Republic that harvest talent and create an environment that immerses the youth in stories of American culture, American promise and opportunity, and most importantly, the success of current countrymen such as Pedro Martinez or Albert Pujols. Creating heroes for the youth of the Dominican Republic fosters an environment of emulation, where the youth are trained to pattern their behaviors after the way that the heroes are marketed to them via television, newspapers, and word of mouth.

Alan M. Klein, in his history of Dominican baseball entitled *Sugarball,* notes that Dominicans perceive success in baseball as signing a contract with one of these academies, because of the symbolic economic significance that a contract provides. He then writes,

> The dangers inherent in the dream of escaping poverty through sport
> are manifest throughout the third world, but they are especially so in
> the Dominican Republic because many people know someone well who
> has "succeeded" in baseball. (59)

As Klein argues, this sense of perception of what constitutes success creates an illusion where the 1300 or so Dominicans earning a life through American baseball (roughly 50 as major league players, others at various minor league levels or in different staff or club positions) seem to be an enormous critical mass, and a newly signed contract seems a pipeline into that system. Baseball tells the story of both economic and social success through aspirations of heading to America.[3]

Recognizing the ways in which these stories are a fiction is not meant, in any way, to detract from the significance or social impact of the accomplishments of individual players in sports history. Generally speaking, the illusion of the sport-as-social-mobility narrative finds its power not in the athletes themselves, but in the ways that other people re-tell these narratives. The rhetoric that transposes an individual athletic accomplishment into an all-American story of overcoming economic hardships and embracing national ideals of equal opportunity is most often disseminated by ideologies that stand to profit from the cultural clout that comes from appropriating such an extensive institution as sport. For example, the "for kids" section of the White House website during George W. Bush's presidential administration created a section entitled "White House Dream Team," which was purportedly "heros [*sic*] who made a significant contribution to America through their dreams, character traits, and choices" The entire list, which in the fiction of the site is ascribed to the decisions of George W. Bush's pet longhorn Ofelia, is comprised of three artists, three authors, three teachers, three "patriots," and six athletes. Four of the six athletes who, in this framework, embody the necessary elements of the narrative have already been mentioned in this chapter: Grange, Clemente, Robinson, and Owens.[4] In short biographies describing the accomplishments of each star, the website attempts to lay out the actions and virtues which qualified the person for the honor.

To demonstrate, a passage on the website about Owens typifies the type of rhetoric used: "The son of a sharecropper and grandson of a slave had shown that hard work, talent and determination made champions." That such a statement appears on the official White House site is not trivial, nor is it insignificant that it was targeted directly to children. The connection between stories of sport and narratives of the American Dream is, at its basic level, an ideology, one that endorses American exceptionalism—in fact, that teaches young Americans to believe in their own unique superiority. Sport used in such a way generates powerful, identificatory nationalism, seen overtly in a figure such as Jesse Owens but also in the stories of figures such as Red Grange, figures who were not just sport stars but "champions." These assumptions serve as a crucial rhetorical device for perpetuating certain social systems and indoctrinating larger populations of spectators. Often history books, sportswriting, radio, television, and Hollywood publicize the notion that by looking at how American sport icons have used sport for social advancement, American citizens can find positive proof of a classless society. After all, the argument might conclude, what other nation could develop such stars? Where else could one find such model examples of realizing the inalienable rights of opportunity and success? The circulation of such ideological-based readings of these athletes histories also reveals another desire of those possessing this ideology—a desire to propagate belief in the contention that if sport embodies the story of America, then America can conversely (and even perhaps needs to) structure itself more like sport. The nation should, so the logic goes, see the "winners and losers" of the nation as rightfully deserving their positions because of what they made out of their equal opportunity rather than attempting to explain social stratification in terms of prejudice and inequality.

This rhetoric is, at its heart, a product of social ideologies, reproduced by institutions that lie outside of the sport. Yet one interesting observation is that ironically, the sports figures appropriated by the American Dream, the "heroes" themselves, sometimes begin to believe in the rhetoric and then invariably recapitulate this myth in their own recounting of their biographical experiences. We've already seen the way that Red Grange told his story as one of a movement from a Huckleberry Finn-like youth to a near millionaire. Sammy Sosa, former Major League baseball star, utilizes similar narrative techniques in his autobiography (published in 2001 at the height of his popularity). Sosa begins his book by detailing his yearly pilgrimage back to San Pedro, driving his sports car through the poverty-stricken streets. In this narrative, his car stops at the run-down baseball field where he first began to play, and he takes out bags and bags of bats, balls, and other baseball equipment, sets them on the field, and puts on a batting practice exhibition as hundreds of locals leave whatever they may have been involved in and gather around him, witnessing him hit towering homeruns over the makeshift left-field fence. As he describes it, "the backstop is a sagging, chain-link fence, and there are no bleachers to speak of. The park is in a modest, working-class neighborhood and is filled with small, barefoot children, just like I used to be" (16). Such an anecdote allows Sosa to narrate a sort of ritualistic remembrance of "where he came from," using sport as the tool for juxtaposing the difference between his life in the United States as a rich, well-known sports idol and the little boy he "used to be."

More importantly, Sosa's language quite visibly reflects the narratives with which he was raised, those of social advancement, economic success, and national progression through baseball. He uses the worn down image of San Pedro's baseball field as a symbol for the conditions which he supposedly escaped: "The field itself is rough compared to the baseball diamonds in America. There are stones all over the infield. The outfield grass is hard and patchy. The dugouts are made of stone and painted green—though the paint has been chipping since I was a kid" (15–16). When he "was a kid," his only social aspirations were his life of shining shoes and having enough food for the entire family living in his one-bedroom apartment. Yet all of this imagery works toward a single purpose within the autobiography; the descriptions of the park and the way things used to be for Sosa are setting for the "children dressed in stained T-shirts and cut-off shorts" (15) who run alongside Sosa's expensive sports car and shout his name.

Sosa continually mentions how he grew up with aspirations to be the next Dominican star, hoping to emulate Roberto Clemente. But more than serving as a descriptor of his athletic ability Sosa's autobiography emphasizes the ways in which baseball helped him support his mother, how baseball led him to the United States, and how baseball resulted in millions of dollars and untold fame. Yet while reinforcing the idea that baseball was the distinctive factor in what would become his economic and social advancement, Sosa also reinscribes the story that people tell about him onto the youth who still live in San Pedro, playing baseball amidst the sagging fence, stony infield, and chipping paint. According to his own narrativization of his history, Sosa implicitly claims that those youth still living in the Dominican Republic, if they want to have any hope to better their own situations, have no choice but to emulate him. Sosa's story of sport is self-serving rather than egalitarian; it works to solidify his own place in the historical chain rather than encourage all Dominican youth to realize their equal opportunities for success.

Ironically, with such structures, with descriptions of the way his sports car "bump[s] along a dirt road that leads to a ragged baseball diamond with no infield grass" (15), Sosa's autobiography actually demonstrates the complete absence of equality, in opportunity or otherwise. And, significantly, the narrative subsumes Sosa the individual athlete. In effect, the narrative of the "American Dream," that which Sosa was inundated with growing up, colonizes him; it overtakes his individuality and uses his success to propagate itself among another generation of the Dominican Republic, thus "colonizing" them, too. Of course, the tragedy is that once that success no longer exists, the cultural narrative, never having any real foundation in reality, finds other objects to hero-ify. Early in 2006 Sosa's career demonstrated this tragedy when, embroiled in steroid suspicion and several years of severely declining performance, Sosa effectively retired by turning down a minor league contract with the Washington Nationals. Brian Smith writes, "[Sosa's] smile and mantra of 'baseball has been very, very good to me' were ubiquitous. And he truly represented the notion that baseball is the sports world's version of the American dream . . . Sosa was held up as a champion of the people when the people needed him and now they don't. It's that simple. In baseball . . . you're only noticed as long as you're useful" (*Vanguard*). Sosa's rapid fall from grace and whimpering exit from the game of baseball is one of the most poignant incriminations of baseball's American Dream narrative and the way this narrative appropriates individuals for its own perpetuation.

In this exploration of the ideology behind the rhetoric of seeing sport as a way to social mobility and all the problems bound up in such an ideology, I have often referred to the phrases "American Dream" and "American exceptionalism" by labeling them as narratives. Perhaps a more appropriate label would be the term "fantasy." The economic and social promises that sport supposedly offers to aspiring youth who emulate the actions they observe in their idols are, in actuality, completely out of reach of nearly all of the would-be Sosas (or, in recent days, Albert Pujolses) in the Dominican Republic. For every Sammy Sosa that makes it to America on a big-league roster, there are literally hundreds of Hispanics who labor in the minor leagues and thousands more who never make it to the United States. This stark fact of reality is in no way limited to baseball or Central American youth; in fact, all the would-be Lebron Jameses in the United States are perhaps even less likely to see the realization of their athletic "American Dream" than the kids in the Dominican. An African-American male growing up in New York City, in terms of statistics, is 10 times more likely to become a doctor or a lawyer than a professional basketball player. Larry Johnson, former NBA star for the New York Knicks, commented upon the rhetoric often surrounding him as an example of an African-American who "escaped" his urban upbringing:

> No one man can rise above the masses of the condition of his people. Understand that. Here's the NBA, full of blacks, great opportunities, they made beautiful strides. But what's the sense of that . . . when I go back to my neighborhood and see the same thing? I'm the only one who came out of my neighborhood. Everybody ended up dead, in jail, on drugs, selling drugs. (Pre-game interview)

The social situation that Johnson identifies in 1990s America, while uniquely dire in the consequences he sees for those who fail at realizing those promises they thought sport would give them, is simultaneously representative of the failure of the American Dream motif from the beginnings of spectator sport culture. In the first decade of the twentieth century, for example, while Babe Ruth was able to garner indescribable celebrity, economic power, and social prestige, untold numbers of youth who had grown up in downtown Baltimore with him lived out their lives within the conditions into which they were born. The statistical hope of ascending the social ladder through sport is, and has historically been, non-existent.

Despite the fiction, however, the power of the fantasy lies in the narratives that we hear and in their reinforcement of the belief of American exceptionalism. Ballparks and sports bars are more and more becoming politically contentious areas in which ideology seems to be trumping history. American culture continues to associate spectator sports with social success and national superiority. Marie Hardin writes that the nation "glorifies tales of the 'rugged individualist' by rejecting interdependence as weak and undesirable" and that "through sport, the body has become a site of struggle over symbolic and material rewards between dominant and subordinate groups" (3.3). With such an abundance of such rhetoric, rhetoric which masks the underlying realities that sport is creating the very hierarchies and stratifications it claims to render obsolete, it's no wonder that George Bush was described as a "tennis-playing, fly-fishing, quail-hunting skull-and-bones Yalie." Sport demonstrates that we *are* divided by class, because it historically and contemporarily plays a vital role in constructing that division on levels extending from local communities to national imaginaries.

Chapter Two
Gridiron Paradise: Princetonian Football, American Class

"There is really much to be said in favor of football, and much has been well said and explains why the sport has acquired its tenacious hold upon players and spectators," writes Walter Camp in *The Book of Football*, published in 1910 as part of his "Library of Sport" series (96). Camp is often referred to as the father of modern football, primarily because of his influence in the evolution of the rules and organization of the sport in the 1890s[1]. His assertion above is typical of the most consistent message that Camp tried to spread about football throughout his life—that football is a game that powerfully, almost hypnotically, appeals to both athletes and fans alike.

Camp later explains his reasoning behind his assertion, arguing that American football's popularity—as well as its benefit to society—is due in large part to its ability to "train" youth; that is, Camp portrays football as a moral and ethical force. "If we teach him to play," continues Camp, "we have some chance to teach him fair play, and as the essence of his training for his games is physical and moral cleanliness, so we are helping him along that road by showing him that the best athlete is the moral athlete" (140). Camp's vision of football was that it had the ability to refine American boys into "men." Of course, Camp's assertions also implicitly argue that if the moral values of "a clean life, practical self-denial, discipline, obedience, unmurmuring pluck, and a good deal of patience" (140) are important for the youth, then they are important for the country itself, as those being trained by college football will be the "reigning" generation once they pass through the initiatory stages of life (where football was, and is, so often played). Through such continual expressions of this rhetoric, Camp's role in the development of college football went much beyond contributions to rules and league formations. As he wrote and spoke about football, his arguments posit football as a game capable of not only instilling an ideology of morality in its athletes and spectators, but also instilling social responsibility. In short, Walter Camp believed that football would—and should—function as an activity that molds youth and, by extension, raise them up as the nation's future leaders.

By and large Camp's declaration of the moral role of football in society was a minority sentiment. More numerous writings, while still recognizing the extent to which society was embracing football, questioned the basis for the popularity of football in American society. A majority of the writing other than Camp's about football critiqued its popularity, centering in some way on the inherent violence of the game. For example, in 1888 the *New York Times* ran a commentary on the Yale-Princeton game which discussed how "the favorite methods of damaging an opponent were to stamp on his feet, to kick his shins, to give him a dainty upper cut, and to gouge his face in tackling" (qtd. in Oriard, *Reading Football* 202). In 1897 the *Evening World* newspaper ran a column for several weeks entitled, "Do You Think Football Is Brutal Sport?" That same year, when a player was crushed to death during a game, the *New York Herald* ran a story demanding reform. In fact, in 1905, President Theodore Roosevelt called representatives from Harvard, Yale, and Princeton together and convinced them that if football didn't become less violent, he would see it outlawed.

Yet Camp refused to admit to the violence or danger of football. Unable to accept such an assessment of the sport, he wrote only of skill and precision, of value and virtue. In fact, perhaps part of Camp's intentions was to turn the rhetoric *away* from the brutality many saw in the game by focusing instead on romanticized descriptions and progressive, instructive values. He composed an annual review/preview of each college football season, detailing which individual plays from individual games he considered worthwhile for the American public to read about. In doing so, he created a culture of taste surrounding football. In Camp's vision, the kicking and running plays were the archetypal symbols of refined taste in football because of their grace, their precision, and their reliance upon athletic talent. By the same token, he despised the "flying wedge," an innovative play first executed in 1892, as nothing more than a mass movement of chaos, as equally likely to be pushed backward as forward (Powel 76). Analogically, the flying wedge was a play with no sense of direction or leadership and hence no real progress, the antithesis of the type of skill that a "moral" youth would be in need of.

Camp's attempts to create a culture of refinement out of playing and watching football are significant. For him, the details of the game itself were vital, because they spoke to what he labeled the "personality in foot-ball" (137), a cultural understanding that not just the players but also the anatomies of the game (the rules, the strategies, etc.) promulgated the ethics of work, discipline, taste, and achievement which comprised his own ideological desires for the direction that society should move in. Camp portrayed a football of refined aesthetics, and felt that the game "has trained faculties that go far to make the successful man"; in other words, that it could create upstanding building blocks for constructing a society (141). His copious writings, his coaching camps and seminars, and even his creation of a yearly "All-American" team can be read as his attempts to control the narrative of football, to shape its cultural impact according to his own motivations.

IVY LEAGUE IDEOLOGIES

Camp's version of the story that football tells was keenly attractive to the personalities allied with American universities such as Harvard, Yale, and Princeton—those universities usually associated with wealth and privilege. The Ivy League[2] schools in which football first grew to prominence were, in the latter part of the nineteenth century and first part of the twentieth century, actively cultivating characters that they wanted as (and believed would become) the future leaders of the country. In doing so, the figures of power in the universities had an investment in seeing that a particular graduating class ascribed to their social ideologies, ideologies which were couched in terms of morality and virtue and which had prospered in earlier generations of these universities' students. In 1913, Princeton president John Hibben gave the graduates a "charge" utilizing language framed within a metaphor of chivalry:

> the world expects you to produce as well as to consume, to add to and not to subtract from its store of good, to build up and not tear down, to ennoble and not degrade. It commands you to take your place and to fight your fight in the name of honor and of chivalry, against the powers of organized evil and of commercialized vice, against the poverty, disease, and death which follow fast in the wake of sin and ignorance, against all the innumerable forces which are working to destroy the image of God in man, and unleash the passions of the beast. There comes to you from many quarters, from many voices, the call of your kind. It is the human cry of spirits in bondage, of souls in despair, of lives debased and doomed. It is the call of man to his brother . . . such is your vocation; follow the voice that calls you in the name of God and of man. The time is short, the opportunity is great; therefore, crowd the hours with the best that is in you. (qtd. in Brooks 4)

There are, of course, unstated repercussions bound up in this metaphor. Most significantly, by invoking images of a Galahad Knight through utilizing the concept of chivalry, Hibben implicates his University in a feudal-like system.

Where Hibben then speaks of ethics and morals, when he compares the Princeton graduate to a chivalric knight, it is imperative to also read that the power which Princeton has bestowed upon these students—power that is, in this case, status, prominence, and prospective national success—was in the hands of a select few who had the 20th century equivalent to royal blood. The majority of the population—the unprivileged masses—live their lives to support the privileges enjoyed by the upper class but are themselves left out of the system. This, naturally, is where the force of a Princetonian system lies. By initiating students, from freshmen to seniors, into the structures of the system through such feudal metaphors, the elite were able to promote ideological assumptions under the name of "values," both justifying their own privilege and ensuring the continuance of the system.

A connection between the Ivy League social system and college football now becomes more apparent. If football, a game still played primarily in the Ivy Leagues through the century's first two decades,[3] was marketed as Camp described—a tasteful, instructive, refining practice—and these institutions had agendas about developing the tastes, values, and mind sets of their students, then the game of football could be used to achieve these goals of the elite population. Camp's assumptions about and numerous writings on the benefits of football to America's youth tell a story about football, a narrative particularly attractive to the major universities playing the game in the first part of the twentieth century. Camp's football is a game where the quarterback, the gallant hero, leads his group of gentlemen attendants to victory. Football could be a training ground, teaching its players to then go on and gallantly lead family, business, and country to "victory" as well, all in the name of the University.

By placing football in such a prominent position in the life of an Ivy League young man, those at the top of the social system are able to avoid challenges to their privileged position in a way not offered by any other cultural institution. As Michael Oriard argues, football

> implied a rule-governed contest in which the better man won through superior merit, affirming a meritocracy that exalted the winners without altogether diminishing the losers . . . [t]o imagine an America shaped by the fair contests of competing individuals offered assurance that those who had power deserved it, those who did not had had their fair chance. (*Sporting With the Gods* 27–28)

Yet this conception of the way that football works, growing out of the appropriation of Walter Camp's narrative of football because it so closely modeled the Ivy League's own narrative of American social class, is paradoxical. The key word in Oriard's statement is "implied." For while football *implies* that everyone starts on equal ground and that the "best" triumph, the game more realistically reinforces the power structures already in place among those playing the game, especially those attending universities of wealthy families' sons throughout the late nineteenth/early twentieth centuries. We could say, then, that Camp's most significant role is not necessarily as the father of college football's rules or even of its mythos as exemplary teacher of the virtuous life. Instead, Camp is the primary influential voice behind football's fantasy of being a sport that encourages the imagination of "fair contests" when it, in actuality, is a means for obscuring the unsustainability of such a claim.

THE CULTURE WITHIN THE WALLS

In 1927 F. Scott Fitzgerald, in an essay appearing in *College Humor,* labeled Princeton University as a "myth, a vision" of America ("Princeton" 103). Fitzgerald matriculated at Princeton only a year after Hibben gave the above cited "chivalry" speech at graduation, and his years at school were saturated with personalities and attitudes both reinforcing and, at times, challenging Hibben's vision for the University. Fitzgerald's years at Princeton, culminating in his dropping out of the university to fight in World War I,[4] is often considered (by Fitzgerald himself and by contemporary scholars) to be the most significant period in terms of formulating his interests in status, class, and nationhood, issues which he would spend a lifetime dissecting through his fiction. Fitzgerald's retrospective comparison, thinking of Princeton as a mythic representation of America, was an important hypothesis for Fitzgerald, for it allowed him to comment not just on the University but also on the nation by exploring an environment with which he was intimately familiar. In doing so, Fitzgerald would reach the conclusion that Princeton was a place "that preserves so much of what is fair, gracious, charming, and honorable in American life" (103).

Yet in the same essay, Fitzgerald also notes that, at Princeton,

> [f]ootball became, back in the nineties, a sort of symbol. Symbol of what? Of the eternal violence of American life? Of the eternal immaturity of the race? The failure of a culture within the walls? Who knows? It became . . . the most intense and dramatic spectacle since the Olympic games. (94)

Encapsulated in Fitzgerald's language about *football* at Princeton is a recognition that the "intense and dramatic spectacle" of football is *not* analogous to a myth or vision of American charm. Instead, he questions to what degree football might represent a "failure," specifically the failure of a culture. Referencing the 1890s, Fitzgerald undoubtedly sees the tensions surrounding football's place in society underscoring his view of Princeton football. It is football, therefore, which helps Fitzgerald express doubt as to the efficacy of analogizing Princeton with the nation.

Fitzgerald's first novel, *This Side of Paradise,* is an exploration into the world of Princeton, and as such is Fitzgerald's first major inquiry into issues of social distinction and social status. It is his attempt to answer the question, "What's prestige, at best?" (121). The experiences of young Amory Blaine within the novel can be read as Fitzgerald's exploration into the "culture within the walls," a culture in which Amory wishes to be "prominent" (49) at school and strives to model himself after the "seldom named, never really admitted," yet pervasively worshiped "Big Man" (47). At the same time, the portrayal of Amory's time at school can be read as Fitzgerald's first investigation of the Princeton-as-America hypothesis. Fitzgerald, in *This Side of Paradise,* considered the lifestyle at Princeton and investigated the degree to which it could be seen as a cultural microcosm for a much larger environment (or, as Isabelle puts it to Amory, "O you and Princeton! You'd think that was the world, the way you talk!" (91)). Amory's experiences in the novel depict the desire that modern American youth had to break into the social world, and as such the novel explores the intricacies of how activities of the Princeton social system, including the "spectacle" of football, correspond with or sit in conflict with the emerging American class stratifications.

The majority of my argument relies upon a cultural conversation. As I work with Fitzgerald's retrospective comments about football at Princeton, and investigate how such assumptions work within the fictional world of *This Side of Paradise,* I will show the ways in which young Fitzgerald provides a more complex response to rhetoric like that of Walter Camp's. If Princeton symbolically represents the American culture, and football a sort of cultural failure, then the implications are clear—something about football, as it was played at Princeton, provided Fitzgerald a language for identifying failures within the Princetonian way of life. Football is the key for seeing the disjunctions Fitzgerald identified even as he attempted to connect the class system at Princeton with the act of living in a much larger America.

Though Fitzgerald is not free of culpability from his own insistence that he deeply desired the social life he imagined at Princeton, *This Side of Paradise* reveals that he was simultaneously critical of his own dreams.

Fitzgerald was, to use Nick Carraway's terms, both within and without the system. Fitzgerald's way of looking at football helps us refine the way we evaluate his way of looking at America. The novel's use of football ultimately emphasizes the notion that Princeton's social systems are *not* representative of the American social landscape. More significantly, *This Side of Paradise*, as a story of football, questions Walter Camp's vision of the game. Fitzgerald demonstrates not only the complexities involved in conceptualizing social class systems saturated with Princeton football players, but also theorizes a dangerous cultural effect that the game of football could have on his young, modern generation. Fitzgerald, perhaps on some level desiring to buy into Camp's vision of what football ought to be, nonetheless reveals some of the dangerous problems inherent in the homogenous demographic make-up of the football-playing student body which Fitzgerald observed and which he so often tried to identify himself with.

Amory's reactions to his first few days of school depict the desire that entering freshmen had to break into the social world, and these reactions set the stage for exploring the intricacies of Princeton's social stratifications. Amory's statement of his goals, though a fictional representation, is quite realistic historically speaking. Upon entering school, all Princeton freshmen were given a copy of the "Freshman Handbook." This pocket-sized, leather-bound book, nicknamed the Freshman Bible, contained the admonition, "Read this little book from cover to cover. Its pages will make you cognizant of things as they are at Princeton. Have a large circle of acquaintances, but go slow in forming intimate friendships" (69). This handbook, this code of socially acceptable behavior which included a list of the most advantageous freshmen activities as well as a list of things freshmen were prohibited from doing, reinforced the social power of such concepts. This guidebook is demonstrative of the social atmosphere surrounding freshmen students, exemplified through such rhetorical statements as, "the following customs are, of course, unwritten laws, but they have grown up with the history of 'Old Nassau.' . . . Anyone who enters into the life of Princeton for the first time will of course desire to observe them" (63). By spelling out social behavior, this handbook helped create a discourse of power. It reinforced the role of emulation, and cemented the figure of the Big Man in the minds of incoming freshmen as if it were a natural role for all to strive to assume. Cultural objects such as the Freshman Handbook relied upon indoctrination to perpetuate the social system—such a phenomenon was very tangible evidence for the feudal-like society of Princeton life. Most students would subsequently recapitulate this social conduct by accepting and adhering to these customs as freshmen and imposing them on succeeding freshmen classes as well.

Observation and emulation are at the core of the idea of The Big Man on Campus. And, traditionally, the figure of the Big Man comes back to Walter Camp's rhetoric concerning football's role in a society. The Big Man was always the football player—Camp's football player of self-discipline, refinement, courage, and by extension power, prestige, and privilege. Two things dominated Princeton life in the early 1900s; football, and striving to be at the top of this "world" which the President described as a feudal hierarchy. And the two, as Camp knew, most often went hand in hand.

> All our schools have learned that the best government is that in which the higher-form boys take the major part, and into that government enters as a large factor the very hero-worship of the small boy for the big boy—the would-be athlete for the school standard-bearer in sport. (140)

Thus in *This Side of Paradise*, Amory, knowing his decision to be prominent at school requires a carefully constructed plan, chooses an activity that best represents his social desires yet which also methodically follows the code established by previous generations of the social system. While other students join the college newspaper staff or become involved with various clubs, Amory asserts that he is "going to take a whack at freshman football" (*TSOP* 44). Amory's choice of activities demonstrates the degree of his aspirations; he doesn't want to be seen as merely "going out for *anything*" (44, emphasis added) but instead "decide[s] to be one of the gods of the class" (47). As a narrative of Princeton life, *This Side of Paradise* thus takes a seemingly minor, almost tangential institution—college football—and makes it central, in that Amory's attempts to succeed at football are a synecdoche within this tale of the possibilities (or impossibilities) of social mobility.

Princeton had a vested interest in teaching incoming freshmen that all the "interest of the fall term centers around the progress of the football team" ("Handbook" 49). In the early 1900s, Princeton already had a football tradition as strong, if not stronger, than the other powerhouse schools they often played. The first recorded college football game had been played in 1869 between Princeton and Rutgers, and year after year the Princeton Tigers were considered among the nation's strongest teams. Because the Princeton football team had such national prominence, athletic success was a matter of university status and pride. Subsequently, the university went to great lengths to market the team in such a way as to ensure the continuation of success:

> The position Princeton has held in the athletic world for many years is too widely recognized to demand special comment . . . four things

unite to bring success—the indomitable Princeton spirit which is never broken by defeat; the democracy of the college life; the impartiality with which all teams are selected and the perfect freedom with which every man with the slightest ability or adaptability for athletics responds to the calls for candidates. ("Handbook" 45).

Moreover, because football was constantly in the forefront of Princeton life, Princeton football games were *the* social events of the year. Socializing overtook watching the game itself, and people were judged socially by who accompanied whom to the games. Additionally, the "Freshman Handbook" contained a lengthy set of instructions on how and why to go out for freshman football, stating that "the best impression that [the class of] 1917 can create in athletics will be to have an unprecedented number of candidates answer the first call" for the football team (45).

HE HAUNTS A WHOLE SCHOOL

While Amory Blaine's decision to play football is certainly significant in considering what *This Side of Paradise* says about the entry into the indoctrinated world of social standing at Princeton, more intriguing is his reaction to the already established hierarchy of football players at Princeton. On his first day on campus, Amory has an experience that provides a glimpse into the way that football controlled the world of privilege and status at Princeton. As this first day winds to a close, Amory sits in solitude on the steps of his just off-campus house and, as if on cue, a song echoes through the towering spires of the nearby campus buildings. Chanting about the glory of the school, a group of singers appears and Amory immediately distinguishes Allenby, "the football captain, slim and defiant" (46). Amory has never met Allenby, yet recognizes him nonetheless. Allenby, the Romantic figure, is already firmly established in the upper echelons of the social circle. The act of Amory recognizing him, then, is a product of Allenby's privileged status, bound up in the collective stories and attitudes about him which entering freshmen would, due to Princeton's very overt emphasis on football, automatically assimilate as part of their initiation into the university's social world. Amory has already expressed his awareness of this phenomenon; an earlier passage in the text describes Amory, that morning, taking a window-shopping stroll along Nassau Street. Glancing from shop to shop, Amory sees Allenby's likeness in a store window montage, where the collection of "athletic photographs" prominently displays Allenby's picture larger than the rest (42). Allenby's image, hanging in a store window, points first to a sense of commodification surrounding his social standing. He becomes not a person or even a character in Amory's mind, but he becomes an object—something to be advertised, something to be acquired. Allenby is marketed, and his commodification is an integral part of the social indoctrination surrounding football at the university. That is, Allenby's athletic prowess has granted him a sort of social fetish value among the people in the microcosm of Princeton, and it is their reactions to him that cement his position not just in the store window but in their representative culture.

Allenby, as is true for most Princeton students of the early twentieth century, has the time and economic means to accommodate an activity such as football. Or, as late nineteenth-century sociologist Thorsten Veblen might say, the time and means to waste. A fundamental aspect of Veblen's analysis is that as a society with the capital, both economic and temporal, to produce waste, the pecuniary class devotes a good deal of its time to war or war-like endeavors (which, for Veblen, is what sports are) rather than productive work (26). This leads him to argue that sports are not about play, but about waste. Veblen was quite critical of college football, claiming that

> the culture bestowed in football gives a product of exotic ferocity and cunning. It is a rehabilitation of the early barbarian temperament, together with a suppression of those details of temperament which, as seen from the standpoint of the social and economic exigencies, are the redeeming features of the savage character. (160)

Because of this connection he sees between a pecuniary culture conspicuously consuming their time and the violent, war-like nature of football, Veblen argues that while football games "are partly simple and unreflected expressions of an attitude of emulative ferocity," they are, more significantly, "activities deliberately entered upon with a view to gaining repute for prowess" (156). In Veblenian terms, this athletic picture of Allenby would represent his prowess, his ability to rise above the rest of the crowds. Or, more accurately, it represents Princeton's desire to place him in that privileged position, selling his prowess in order to accumulate its own status. Being placed at the center of the store montage of athletic photographs makes Allenby the perfect picture of the pecuniary class.

Moreover, the intangible "status" the store advertises through Allenby is not connected to his athletic accomplishments but to his relationship with the culture of Princeton. The language of the text reveals only that the photograph is one of "Allenby, the football captain." The two titles appear as one phrase as if it were all part of his name; "football captain" is an appellation describing part of his (commodified) identity rather than his activities.

Bound up in the label "captain" are notions of prestige, notions of popularity, notions of social status among his teammates, coaches, and especially the fans. It is less a signifier of his athletic achievements (though they would have been a contributing factor) and more a signifier of his social ones. Thus the act of calling him "Allenby, the football captain," with the two phrases inseparable from each other, equates Allenby the character with these social connotations. The text is, in effect, calling him "Allenby the esteemed," "Allenby the elite," "Allenby the 'Big Man.'" Allenby is everything that Walter Camp would hope football could produce.

Additionally, the scene relies on the fact that the photograph, in establishing Allenby's social prominence, is set up in the store window so others can observe him. For his image to have any type of concrete social influence, it must be observed by someone standing outside the store. There must be a spectator for it to have an effect. The fact that the photograph is "athletic" suggests that Allenby is pictured in a graceful or deft football maneuver. The interaction between Amory and the photograph is therefore a representation of the relationship between a fan and a player; Amory watches, while Allenby plays.

Significantly, the fact that it is a picture also marks the situation as a visual representation and calls attention to the fact that it is not real. Whether it was a live action shot or a posed action shot (which would have been more likely given technological limitations and the fact that sports photography didn't take off until after World War I) is irrelevant; it is still a photograph, in which Allenby is frozen in an instant, preserving his social standing in the minds of those looking at him. Moreover, the portrayal of his supposed skill is in iconic rather than actual form; that is, Amory's (and the reader's) first encounter is with an image rather than a person actually practicing on a field. In this, the text is able to reinforce that Allenby's behavior is not the source of his status. Instead, his status comes from the way he looks, from the way he is marketed—it comes from how people react to and interpret what they perceive as his behavior.

Metaphorically, it is a product of a rhetorical situation, relying upon a reciprocal interaction between his actions and the spectator's observations. Amory's small act of observation underscores the role that spectatorship plays in social construction; Allenby plays well on the field, and the fans enjoy his success and reward him accordingly. But importantly, spectatorship also leads to a form of identification and vicarious status. The picture signifies that Allenby's success then becomes *their* (the Princeton fans, and Princeton itself) success, at least in the sense that the Freshman Handbook describes what Princeton athletics means for the status of Princeton's students among individuals outside the walls. This relationship is reinscribed by the iconic creation of the second interaction between the fan and the football captain that I referenced earlier. What Amory ultimately recognizes later that night amidst the singing crowd is not Allenby, but "Allenby-ness"; he can sense the social cult of Allenby and what it means for him to be connected to this community by virtue of watching and admiring. Amory feels once again, in the "infinitely transient" song (46), the same ungraspable, yet certainly desirable, status that was earlier advertised as something that outside observers need to acquire, need to obtain, need to construct themselves. It is images like this that made football such a nucleus of social standing. Football spectatorship encourages social emulation, reinforcing that one's role in attending Princeton was to support the system in hopes of someday occupying that Big Man position.

Allenby himself, as many Fitzgerald biographers have noted, was modeled on the historical figure of Hobey Baker. Baker, the captain of both the Princeton football and hockey teams, occupied a social position at the university similar to that which Fitzgerald paints in the figure of Allenby. He was the Big Man on Campus during the second decade of the twentieth century. George Frazier, a classmate of Baker's, recalled that "the aura of Hobey Baker permeated the campus" (Hobey Baker Papers). Fitzgerald, having met Baker just one time, categorized him as "an ideal worthy of everything in my enthusiastic admiration, yet consummated and expressed in a human being who stood within ten feet of me" (qtd. in Davies 135). Named to a series of all-American teams, including Walter Camp's 1913 team, Baker was often called an athlete who was "used to being a hero" (*Brooklyn Daily Eagle*, Hobey Baker Papers).

Yet despite the idealism that Fitzgerald might have read about or seen encapsulated in Baker's playing abilities, he also would have been aware of the degree to which Baker was portrayed as more than an exemplary sports star. Though Baker was a prominent and gifted athlete, his "aura" at Princeton was due not so much to his athletic achievements as it was to his supposed refined behavior and his elite social standing. The Princeton of Baker's time was cognizant it was striving to cultivate a sense of an elite class and, as Brooks writes,

> aimed to take privileged men from their prominent families and toughen them up, teach them a sense of social obligation, based on the code of the gentleman and noblesse oblige. In short, it aimed to instill in them a sense of chivalry. (3)

Baker, competing at a school with such a goal, was described as playing in a "world in which young men soared into the sky and fell in flames. There was such gallantry, such great grace in that world" (Hobey Baker Papers). Baker's athletic accomplishments are framed as the epitome of the chivalric metaphor so often applied at the Ivy Leagues, with descriptions of his games often described as epic battles and he as the Galahad knight, a model for young men to aspire to be like. John Tunis wrote that Baker, never wearing a helmet, made "the whole atmosphere electric" and stuck out as a god among men on the football field (qtd in Fimrite 135). Moreover, Baker, in keeping with the sense of social privilege that his position of "captain" would warrant, was heralded as not just being a sportsman but of being a "gentleman's sportsman." Stories written about him often described his athletic play with words such as "dignified" and "mannered." His biographer, John Davies, notes that Baker lived up to the status of his athletic role, having only two penalties called on him and often seeking out opposing players to thank them for good games. The rhetoric surrounding the historical figure of Hobey Baker was adequately summed up in 1962 by George Frazier, who wrote that "he haunts a whole school, and from generation unto generation. You say 'Hobey Baker,' and all of a sudden you see the gallantry of a world long since gone" (Hobey Baker Papers).

Fitzgerald, modeling Allenby after Baker, was interested not merely in a concrete historical reference or even in grounding his text in historical details, but in tapping into Baker's cultural narrative as a way to develop his thematic agenda. At Princeton, Baker held a social position that was reinforced in the eyes of his classmates by the constant re-inscription of his status as "the football captain" in the minds of the University's other students. He could not haunt the school without the fans themselves, those who had made him a school hero and those who insisted in trying to model themselves after him. Yet it wasn't his playing ability, masterful though it might have been; it was the very fact that the game of football was marketed as an object of status. Fitzgerald, experiencing a Princeton surrounded by "the aura" of Hobey Baker (whose middle name, incidentally, was Amory) and desiring to portray such concepts of athletic success as a sign of social standing, thus knew that Baker needed to figure into *This Side of Paradise*. Allenby is not Hobey Baker in the sense of him being a historical figure, but is instead a representation of the social type that Baker was; Allenby is a demonstration of the connection between football and the Princetonian society surrounding Amory or Fitzgerald or other Princeton students, real or imagined.

In language that foreshadows Jay Gatsby's later pursuit of Daisy Buchanan in *The Great Gatsby*, Amory, closing his eyes in order not to disturb the "rich illusion of harmony," wants to "ramble through the shadowy scented lanes" (47). Just as Gatsby's aspirations involve social status more than economic accumulation, the relationship in *This Side of Paradise*—between football star and football spectator—is about social position instead of athletic ability. The historical Hobey Baker, in fact, came from a family with limited financial wealth but renowned societal standing. And though the passage in which Amory sees Allenby is not about economics in the concrete sense, it is about status; football provides a language for talking about social mobility. Football, on one level, leads to a particular incarnation of the American Dream, one that bestows communal adulation and devotion. The marching, singing phalanxes are a form of social capital, and Amory looks to Allenby as his exemplar and guide to reaping social rewards, reacting to the athletic celebrity by sighing in fascination at the sight of the ideals Allenby supposedly represents. It is such reactions that make Allenby's commodified status so powerful. Allenby represents Amory's social desires; he is the type of "god" that Amory wants to become, literally believing that physical emulation will lead to social emulation. Veblen sees this relationship as another fundamental aspect of the game of football. In addition to functioning as a symbolic sign of waste, football for Veblen is also about pecuniary emulation—not just wasting social capital, but modeling one's self after those who do. Amory, feeling it will help him garner the social status he perceives in a fetishized figure such as Allenby, participates in football as a way of participating in the pecuniary class.

Despite this, Amory is anxiously aware that he is not on a par with "the football captain" and is instead merely a member of the mass following at this time (*TSOP* 47). Being the football captain, whether such a condition is bound up in that store photograph or in the textual descriptions and cultural narrative of Hobey Baker, elicits the worship of those typified by Amory or by the marching phalanx rhythmically following behind Allenby. Yet the condition of being the football captain also makes apparent the different roles that an Amory figure or a marching mass plays. Amory sees his identity as a member of the "big-game crowds" (49) as a representation of class standing. He sees a distinction, drawn along the lines of football, in which the populous masses, those who watch instead of play, are separated from the upper classes of the "Big Man." These upper classes are not represented in groups in the way that the middle class of the marching phalanx is; instead, Allenby alone stands in for an entire privileged class. While I've mentioned how he is portrayed as a sort of type, he is also an amalgamic representation, an encapsulation of the elite, a composite figure that provides a very tangible person around whom the middle classes can rally and whom they can aspire to emulate. In mediating between the members of the indiscernible faces of the phalanx and the face of Allenby, Amory senses, in this one moment, the tensions of the Princetonian class system. Amory, in "all the air of struggle that pervaded his class" (47), cultivates from this encounter his own dreams of heroic status after the manner of Allenby in an aim to separate himself from the big-game crowds. He wants to be a player rather than a mere fan—thus his earlier assertion that playing freshman football will turn him into a god of the class.

Thus, through representations of football at Princeton, Fitzgerald is beginning to raise the questions that would haunt him throughout the rest of his fiction, questions about the structures of such a dream and the figures that might make it possible. Yet despite the transcendental mythos of Amory's encounter here with Allenby, Fitzgerald also questions the efficacy of such an aspiration. The supposed American Dream that Princeton football promises (here in embryonic form), the "culture within the walls" that supposedly offers a social mobility through success on the gridiron, in actuality defines the boundaries of its upper class as limited, unpassable to individuals lying outside of the elite. After all, the pane of glass allowing Amory to view Allenby's athletic photograph from Nassau Street may be transparent, but it is also impermeable. Metaphorically, it signifies that the iconic montage is completely exclusive; it is observable but not touchable. Indeed, Amory never even attempts to enter the store. Moreover, Amory doesn't realize that the only accepted form of emulation lies in spectatorship; it relies upon a sense of *vicarious* participation, as if spectators can play alongside their heroes by sitting in the crowds or joining in pep rallies but not on the field. The phalanx of singers following behind Allenby represent a coalescence of status seekers, simultaneously giving Allenby his privileged status and hoping to amass similar status themselves, but reinforcing the barriers. Amory "resent[s] social barriers as artificial distinctions," but quickly learns that despite their synthetic nature, the social distinctions of a world such as Princeton are nonetheless impenetrable; football is key in the social distinctions which, in the same feudal metaphor found throughout the portrayal of football (and Princeton) by various cultural voices, barriers "made by the strong to bolster up their weak retainers and keep out the almost strong" (*TSOP* 47). Once again we see the comparison between football and an age of chivalry, a comparison that is paradoxical on two levels. The first irony lies in the fact that the genteel, refined images of a chivalric age shouldn't, when logically thought out, merge well with a game so violent and physically brutal as football. Perhaps this is why Camp sought to downplay the violence of the game in the way that he did. Yet at the same time, by requiring such levels of physical strength, football is able to utilize that physicality to hoard social strength. In conjunction with this, the second visible paradox in the feudal analogy lies in the logic of the meritocracy story itself as it relates to football. What Fitzgerald begins to identify as the failure of the culture within the walls is that rather than training boys to be conscientious, socially responsible citizens, football selects those already typical of whom those "at the top" consider to be leaders and uses concepts of observation and emulation to keep others in line with the system. There is no social mobility, only stories of mobility. Along these lines, Amory, days after his romanticized dream-encounter with Allenby, wrenches his knee in practice and is thus "forced to retire" (48). Amory is kept in check by physical limitations, unable to become a football star himself.

THE DAMNED MIDDLE CLASS

This last plot detail requires deeper consideration; if, as earlier asserted, the status of the Princeton football hero is not about the ability to actually play well but instead about the labels, icons, and attitudes surrounding it, it may seem contradictory that Amory's physical limitations prevent him from achieving social status. Couldn't he rely upon garnering social affluence in some other form instead? The answer lies in the University's reactions to Amory's accident. Whereas Allenby, in all that he does, is photographed and advertised as being the "captain," that is, the discourse helps create his status, Amory, before his injury, is instead merely "paragraphed in corners of the 'Princetonian'" (48). He is not being displayed, he is not being watched; the forum through which people can observe Amory is merely a written one. Without the spectacle of athleticism (whether of an actual game or of seeing a visual representation as in Allenby's athletic photograph), there is no sense of fanship, no sense of a crowd, and hence no vicarious participation. People just read about him, without feeling as if they are a part of his success. And without spectatorship, there is no desire for emulation. Furthermore, Amory is represented in the newspaper not as a feature article but as filler material, paragraphed in a corner as if his presence in the textual space functions solely as a way to even up the columns. He isn't accepted into the world of being marketed or being adored. Amory's physical limitations here hence serve as metaphors for cultural ones, and the wrenching of his knee becomes just a part of being "damned middle class" (49). Amory believes that if he cannot play football, he is no better off than those indistinguishable faces that are marching behind Allenby.

Unable to compete on the gridiron, the ambitious Amory is left to "consider the situation" of his social position. Amory still desires to achieve status, to achieve "the being known and admired" (48). He still has dreams of modeling himself after those social characteristics he latched onto in the character of Allenby. The text, after establishing football as a sign of social position and elitism, leaves the discourse of football and begins talking about other institutions at Princeton. Specifically, Amory contemplates participating in the system of eating clubs guiding upper-class life, being on the board of the *Daily Princetonian* newspaper, or joining the Triangle Club theater troupe—all social endeavors that had seemed, to Amory, less ambitious before and only become options once the doors to the social world that football promised were closed. In turning away from football and to activities such as the student paper, a freshman such has Amory would have likely been heavily influenced, once again, by the codified rhetoric of the "Freshman Handbook." The handbook, again emphasizing the importance of engaging in some form of community-forming activity as a way to reap social rewards, stated,

> Every entering man feels ambitious to enter some undergraduate activity. The publications hold a place of high importance, respect, and influence in social life and offer opportunities for the energies of men who do not possess athletic ability. (58)

It would not have been acceptable for a Princeton student to do nothing; all were expected to ingratiate themselves into Princetonian society through one means or another. Yet the words of the handbook, as well as the sequence of choices that young Amory makes, demonstrates a hierarchy in terms of a given activity's prominence. In effect, there is a strata of social life in Princeton's feudal system, signified by one's extracurricular activities. Try out for football first; if you do not "possess athletic ability," drop down a level and try out for *The Princetonian*. The social ladder is painted, and distinctions between positions clearly defined.

VOICES OF DISSENT: SOCIAL VS. SOCIALISM

Significantly, the novel's character of Kerry Holiday serves as a divergent voice to all of Amory's social aspirations, beginning first and foremost with Amory's desire to play football. Kerry functions as an anomaly at Princeton, a critic of the rigid social system and the class tension it creates. As such, he gives voice to Fitzgerald's critical eye, complicating the seemingly simple picture which the "Freshman Handbook" paints about Princeton's social life and revealing, in a way that Amory's early experiences with Allenby cannot, some of the inherent problems that the system of spectatorship, emulation, and "Big Man" worship creates. A self-proclaimed outsider by choice, Kerry "chide[s Amory] gently for being curious . . . about the intricacies of the social system" (*TSOP* 48). After hearing Amory confess that he does not "mind the glittering caste system" as long as he gets to be on top (50), Kerry engages Amory in a series of conversations in which he attempts to identify a structural fallacy in Amory's aspirations for social mobility. When Amory claims that he still wishes to be "prominent," Kerry deridingly calls Amory a "sweaty bourgeois" (50). In other words, Kerry recognizes that Amory buys into the concept that social status is something you can achieve through pro-active effort—Amory wants to bring a girl to the prom and "be damn debonaire about it—introduce her to all the prize parlor-snakes and the football captain" (51), and thus garner status that way. Amory's goals of social mobility hinge upon the results accomplished by exercising his social agency. By calling such a mind set "bourgeois," then, Kerry Holiday is, in effect, telling Amory that working at being prominent will never place someone in the "aristocracy," so to speak; he is trying to get Amory to see that one's actions very often do not correspond with one's social positions, and status is not something that the Big Man such as Allenby needs to earn.

Though not explicit textually, such a goal is especially connected to Amory's desires to physically emulate Allenby. Football is a game all about the result; the final score, the winning team, the hero of the game. Because Amory finds himself in a position where he is unable to achieve the athletic results of a football player, it is almost as if he feels that parroting the other outward signs of elitism—doing what the big man on campus does off the field—will garner the same sort of acceptance. Yet Kerry criticizes this paradigm as misguided, warning Amory that he is "just going around in a circle" (51). Kerry's choice of words here is vital. By describing Amory's aspirations as circular—a movement antithetical to any sort of progress—Kerry acknowledges that class lines are drawn in such a way as utterly to prohibit mobility from one level to another. Amory's endeavors, in attempting to climb the social ladder, instead follow a flat plane, leading him back to where he began. In effect, Kerry provides an ideological voice speaking out against class systems in general; he knows that struggling for social mobility just reinforces Amory's own position as an outsider. Such an ideological position maintains that actions will not cultivate status, but that status is somehow innate. All of Amory's aspirations for social mobility are wrapped up in a sense of defeated movement, and Amory's dreams themselves are what keep him firmly locked in the middle class.

MOVING UP

Interestingly enough, as the novel progresses, Amory does appear to achieve a few of the outward signs of social status. His "arrival," his ability to finally socialize with "the minor snobs" (after realizing that the world of football stardom would never be attainable), is eventually realized "by way of the Princetonian" (72). He sits on the editorial board of the school paper and is able to function partially in the social world as he has been striving to do. His successes are a significant temptation, endowing Amory with a bit of social capital, encouraging him to continue his status climbing. Yet this picture of Amory's petty successes is strategically placed in the novel, after his early conversations with Kerry Holiday, in order to complicate what seems to be an example of social mobility. First and foremost, Amory's achievements are not the athletic ones that he earlier desired. As he is gradually separated from the influence of the sport on life at Princeton, his experiences, while still efforts to model himself after the elite class, more directly expose the problematics of the "Big Man" mind set. In fact, as Amory removes himself from the football culture, he begins to develop within himself complex ideological oppositions to a system of class built around elitism and status. Outside of the cult of Allenby, Amory's paradigm of the social world is challenged, and he responds by listening even more to Kerry's opposing viewpoints and subsequently questioning the degree to which class lines are mutable, not just at Princeton but in the national society as a whole.

The first moment in which Amory gets a sense of this predicament— that he, too, is frozen in his social position, just as Allenby is frozen in the photograph in the store window—is in his experience joining an eating club near the end of his sophomore year. The novel's portrait of the upper-class club organization begins to reveal how the ideological system at Princeton encouraged social climbing among those without "status," yet ultimately denied elite standing to those striving to compete. These clubs, with names such as "Ivy," "Cottage," "Tiger," "Cap and Gown," and "Colonial," were established at Princeton as a forum of "association . . . for social, intellectual and recreative purposes" and had long been supported by both students and administration alike (Eating Club Records). President John Hibben was an ardent supporter of keeping the clubs part of the status quo. In short, the eating clubs were almost as much a fixture of social assembly as the football program was.

Amory longs for the sociability of the clubs, described by the text with phrases such as "detached and breathlessly aristocratic," "broad-shouldered and athletic," "politically powerful" (*TSOP* 48–49). Yet when the time comes for sophomores to join the clubs, in the competition called "March bicker" (Daniel 14), Amory watches "his suddenly neurotic class with much wonder" (*TSOP* 73). Fitzgerald's depiction of the bicker in *This Side of Paradise* is a faithful account of the historical practices, in which students would ask for invitations to certain clubs and the club leadership would make their decisions and issue the invitations. The eating clubs—which were nothing more than off-campus dining halls—determined one's circle of association for the span of the upper-class years. As Amory thus witnesses an "orgy of sociability," he particularly notes that some people "felt themselves stranded and deserted" and even "talked wildly of leaving college" when the "wielders of the black balls"—those controlling the selection process of the system— make their selections of inclusion or exclusion (73).

As was the case when looking at the cultural world of Princeton football, Fitzgerald was both caught up in exploring how one attempts to move up the social ladder through the eating clubs, as well as criticizing it for its inflexible and rigid boundaries. Membership in the prominent clubs was the next best thing to being a football star, but it was not the same lifestyle nor did it engender the same cultural recapitulation that the encouraged emulation of football players would. Though Amory is selected to join Cottage Club (as was Fitzgerald) and he celebrates his sort of social success with a night of partying, mixing and mingling, and self-congratulatory conversation, the passage describing the selection process is immediately followed by a description of another conversation between Amory and Kerry Holiday. Kerry continues to play the role of anti-socialite and continues to voice opposition to the ideology of Princeton's rigid social lines. When Amory, Kerry, and others skip class one afternoon for a road trip to Asbury, they specifically seek out the "most imposing hostelry in sight" at which to eat lunch (76). This dining room serves as a reminder of the eating clubs, which strove to be architecturally impressive as a sign of their importance or reputation. Yet after lunch, instead of reinforcing the symbolic representation of an eating club, Kerry attempts to subvert it. Kerry, claiming their eighteen dollar bill is a "rotten overcharge" (76), responds with a two dollar payment. His is a symbolic act of defiance as well as solidarity among his friends; especially in light of the recent club elections, he is in effect arguing that the sociability of the eating clubs is too taxing to allow for real personal interaction.

Kerry's actions, set up as Amory's first glimpse at an alternative to the Princetonian social system ruled by the football players and eating club presidents, are "a last desperate attempt . . . to fight off the tightening spirit of the clubs" (78–79). Invoking the ideology of the proletariat, Kerry turns to Amory following his act of defiance and remarks, "we're Marxian Socialists . . . we're putting it to the great test" (77). Kerry's rhetoric here speaks not just to Amory, but to the overall ideology of social positioning which Fitzgerald identifies at Princeton, and these two scenes—Amory's election to a club and Kerry's declaration of socialism—are juxtaposed in a way that reveals the complexities of the social world itself. Amory is not ready to yet relinquish the vision of the "perfect type of aristocrat" which Princeton was striving to nurture (78), yet feels persuasively drawn to Kerry as well as to Kerry's brother Burne, who will soon put Kerry's language of embryonic Marxism into action.

PULLED FROM BOTH ENDS

Amory's subjection to ideological rhetoric from these opposing viewpoints demonstrates the difficulty in trying to easily use terms such as "dominant cultural values" or in trying to label the class someone might belong to. The tensions in Amory's social education complicate the feudal-like portrayal of the Big Man/spectator system that we earlier saw in the world of Princeton football. On one hand, students went to Princeton as rich men's sons and were indoctrinated with a sense of their supposed privilege and status within the larger community of the nation. Princeton president Hibben, whose yearly speeches seemed reincarnations of previous ones, challenged the graduating class of 1915 by asking,

> Who will prove that the spirit of peace may become the spirit of valor, and assure the solidarity and progress of our nation? Who but the choice men of our land,—the men of exceptional privilege, who by a process of natural selection have passed from one degree of excellence to another in the arduous discipline of mind and character through years of preparation for a life of service. (qtd. in Brooks 3)

Such language relates privilege to success and even national progress, justifying it with phrases of natural law. Amory feels the allure of this rhetoric, a rhetoric typical of many emerging American nationalist voices that endorsed an underlying sense of social hierarchy. Ideologies such as these would be an extremely powerful influence on the minds of young Princeton students such as Amory, reinforcing the system as students first become "satellites . . . attaching themselves to the more prominent" (*TSOP* 49), and then occupying those positions themselves through a sort of social investiture. And all of Amory's plans for his rise to prominence, for being one of the "hot cats" (50), are a manifestation of the ease with which the social system at Princeton controlled behavior. By invoking natural selection, Hibben could also re-emphasize physical strength and prowess, couching his ideology of social privilege in the myth that a football athlete has won his status fair and square because of his ability. This is why football was such a marketed activity at Princeton.

The community Princeton was trying to cultivate hinged on having very visible "prominent" members. The football captain is the supposed end result, the sort of figure that the Princeton way of life can create, physically as well as socially. And the recapitulation of the social system, the affirmation of this privilege, is facilitated through the act of spectatorship and subsequent emulation. Because the status of a football star, as already established, is based in adulation from those watching rather than those playing, lines of difference are held intact. The distinction between fan and player is the key to both assimilation and exclusion.

But paradoxically, Amory's social successes in the eating clubs are what provide an impetus for losing a bit of faith in the hierarchies of Princeton. The eating clubs are not football, and more importantly are not based in emulation of a select few "types" of success. The eating clubs do not provide markers of individual achievement for the students at Princeton; instead they are more representative of classes than of privileged characters. With the images of Allenby removed from his mind, Amory is able to briefly wonder if Kerry's Marxian socialism might be a more viable alternative.

Marx, whom Fitzgerald once called one of only two "modern philosophers that still manage to make sense in this horrible mess" (*Letters* 290),[5] provides an intriguing lens for responding to the social system at Princeton—especially the club selection process through which Amory has just undergone. This is especially true in light of the sort of "revolt" which Kerry Holiday's brother Burne initiates among the members of the various eating clubs. Burne, claiming that "a logical result if an intelligent person thinks long enough about the social system" would be to abolish the clubs (116), sets off an insurgence which eventually leads to one-third of the junior class resigning from the clubs.[6] Burne's rhetoric of social revolt and "the intense power" and "intense earnestness" with which he speaks (117) becomes just as alluring to Amory as the vision of social nobility Amory identified in Allenby. Burne is not considered a Big Man on campus; he is an anomaly, an outsider. Yet for Amory, he is as much a figure of influence as any Big Man. Burne is the ideological opposition to Allenby, creating a tense dialectic in Amory's attempts to be a part of Princeton's social world. The theoretical forces pulling on Amory reveal that Princeton, for all its emphasis on elitism and class lines and for all the promises that football stardom offers, might not hold all the answers for the society that he will enter upon graduation. Amory begins to wonder if Burne stands "vaguely for a land [he] hoped he was drifting toward"; he mentally postulates that his role in the larger, national culture might be better served by an ideology such as socialism than by the "blindly idling" lifestyle of Allenby's leisurely elitism that he's been aspiring to for two years at Princeton (117).

Despite the conspicuous absence of football in Amory's relationships with the Holiday brothers, Burne Holiday does attend one football game. Phyllis Styles, the "prom-trott[ing]" student who uses all manner of manipulation just to get invited on dates to football games, corners Burne and convinces him that they are going to the Harvard-Princeton game together (120). Burne, demonstrating he perfectly understands the issues of status and social acceptance surrounding the game's attendance as well as the culture of being a fan, subsequently embarks upon a plan to ridicule Phyllis for so overtly buying into the system of spectatorship as it relates to social standing. He shows up to the game "arrayed to the last dot like the lurid figures on college posters" (120). Turning the marketing and commodification of football to his own use, Burne, along with compatriot Fred Sloane, makes himself up in the image of the ideal Princeton fan:

> They had bought flaring suits with huge peg-top trousers and gigantic padded shoulders. On their heads were rakish college hats, pinned up in front and sporting bright orange-and-black bands, while from their celluloid collars blossomed flaming orange ties. They wore black arm- bands with orange 'P's' and carries canes flying Princeton pennants, the effect completed by socks and peeping handkerchiefs in the same color motifs. On a clanking chain they led a large, angry tomcat, painted to represent a tiger. (120–21)

Burne's ploy is not just to embarrass Phyllis; he is satirizing the entire crowd. With his mass accumulation of all the signs of spectatorship, from school colors to school mascots, Burne's message is one of ironic judgment of his fellow fans. Certainly, of course, Burne stands out precisely because of the quantity and degree of his performance; his satire takes typical fanship to its logical extreme. Such an action is designed to demonstrate the ludicrousness of even the most modest show of spectatorship. What Burne knows is that mass spectatorship is a form of vicarious participation; the cheers, the clothes, and the colors are symbols of the crowd's attempt to play alongside their heroes on the field. The mascot, supposedly representing the ferocity of the players, is more of a totem for the fans, another level of worship that they adopt so as to feel more united with the gallant heroes they are upholding through their bestowal of social status. Burne's ironic assumption/appropriation of the commodified image of the football fan is his method for mocking the faith of the fans in the fan/hero relationship. His irony is doubled when half of the crowd "had no idea that this was a practical joke but thought that Burne and Fred were two varsity sports showing their girl a collegiate time" (121).

THE BODIES OF IDEOLOGY

Interestingly enough, as was the case in Amory's adoration of Allenby, his attraction to Burne is not based so much in events such as this as it is in what Burne stands for. Burne does not just espouse a particular ideology; he is the ideology. That is, Burne, too, is a "type"; he is a representation of a class (or in this case, an anti-class) that provides another figure for Amory to imitate. Even in critiquing the world of spectatorship or social climbing, Burne is earning his own following. This consistent emphasis on the personages of class tension rather than merely the ideas they advocate is the real key to understanding the connection between football, a physical game that invites ardent spectatorship, and the resulting status and community of social emulation. In every case, from Amory's worship of the Big Man to his discipleship to Kerry/Burne, the text places at the forefront individual subjects with real bodies and minds, and emulation is situated not nearly as much in the ideology one promotes as in the bodies one follows. To this end, in exploring the social status that eludes aspiring characters such as Amory, the text often utilizes language of biology in order to give exclusion, especially athletic exclusion, more of a "natural" justification in the way that we saw Hibben discussing earlier. Moreover, in doing so the novel traverses the gap between the walls of Princeton and the larger American nation. The text produces, through exploration of the intersections between class and physical composition—including race—that are bound up in football, a more complete picture of how this dramatic spectacle is a failure of not just the Princeton culture, but the national one.

Let's return to an earlier passage, the one in which Amory first sees the athletic photograph of Allenby. Following this significant iconic encounter, with the fresh image of Allenby's "hundred-and-sixty pounds" in his mind (a robust amount for early college football), Amory then walks to the next store and orders a "double chocolate jiggah" from the "colored person" working behind the counter (42). The text is, on one level, emphasizing a shift along class lines, moving from a picture of leisure to a picture of work. Yet there is quite obviously more going on than mere class distinction between these two images. Allenby's status as a figure of leisure might not be so starkly visible were his photograph not immediately juxtaposed with Amory's face-to-face encounter with a working class African-American. The text, in moving along the axis of class, is also moving along that of race, from white to black. The differences in class positions are thus centered in racial ones. Allenby, the white, upper-class football hero, is pictured engaging in a leisure activity, conspicuously consuming time as he functions as an object of spectacle and of mass culture. The African-American is the working class, the figure of labor whose role is not to become mass culture or leisurely to consume time, but merely to dispense mass culture to others for their own consumption. The racial language is not necessarily a metaphor, but a palimpsestic rhetoric; racial difference is superimposed upon social difference. For Amory and his aspirations, a position requiring actual work of any kind is the least envied social position, and the skin color of the confectionery worker thus becomes a sign of undesirability. Being "working class" instead of being a football player would be like being "colored."

Because Amory has his transcendent moment later that night, witnessing Allenby marching through the campus, the text further reinforces the way that upper-class status is coded along racial lines. Before catching a glimpse of the football captain, Amory sees the mass movement of the phalanx accompanying him. Amory notes that it is a "white-clad" phalanx, composed of figures garbed in "white-shirt[s]" and "white-trouser[s]" (46). Amory subconsciously perceives in the phalanx that the unifying force is homogenous color. In their attempts to participate with Allenby, to model themselves after him and attain his social status, the marching supporters use not uniforms or school colors (which were the traditional ways of identifying with a football team), but purely white clothes. Due to such a stark white body of people, contrasting with the darkening sky, Amory notices that the faces are "indistinct," yet the procession stands out amidst the "shadowy" twilight (46–47). With a mass of whiteness behind him, Allenby the football captain marches through the campus "as if aware that this year the hopes of the college rested on him" (46), hopes which are intertwined inextricably in a language of color.

The fact that color would figure so prominently in Amory's first encounter with the social world of Princeton football is to be expected. This particular rhetoric is related to a growing curiosity among Princeton students, Fitzgerald included, in issues of heredity and social Darwinism,[7] especially as they related to social progress. For example, much of the discourse of Hobey Baker's accomplishments was bound up in language of race as a way to figure the lines of the social class to which he belonged as rigid and immutable. Portrayals of Baker as an upper-class gentleman were generally applied as he was compared to his two major contemporaries in the sporting world, Native American Jim Thorpe and African American Jack Johnson, both of whom lived their athletic lives opposite forces similar to the "white platoon" that the fictional Allenby was leading. An article in *The Sporting News* wrote that, as "the gentleman sportsman" and "an inspiration to almost everyone who came in contact with him," Baker was much different than the "Jim Thorpes or Jack Johnsons of his era"[8] (Hobey Baker Papers). What's more, sportswriting of the time consistently focused not just on Baker's abilities or his manners, but on his physical nature and looks, especially in terms of blood and color. A *Brooklyn Daily Eagle* article entitled "Being a Hero is Nothing New to Hobart Amory Hare Baker" wrote that Baker's heroic status relied on him being "the clean cut, light-haired boy . . . [who] was an ideal example of an American Youth" (Hobey Baker Papers). John Davies called him a "flawless instance" of a "rare human breed," someone who could be "called in the biological or genetic sense a 'sport'" (135). John R. Tunis emphasized how Baker "never wore a headguard in football" and so, consequently, everyone only remembers "that great shock of blond hair" (qtd. in Davies 135).

Tunis also wrote a column in which he witnessed a Princeton game played in the rain. Conditions were so terrible that the majority of the contest was played in piles of mud so thick that soon players from both teams were saturated beyond recognition. Tunis made it a point to describe this scene as one in which the mud had "obliterated even the colors distinguishing friend from foe . . . but in the stands everyone knew that shock of yellow hair" (qtd. in Davies 171). Jennie Hibben, the wife of Princeton's president, even remembers shutting her eyes during the game and murmuring, "I just hope that golden-haired boy doesn't get killed!" (qtd. in Davies 171). Fitzgerald's novel, by invoking Hobey Baker, is not just relying on Hobey Baker's "aura" but also on the discourse of color and biology surrounding Baker's athletic endeavors. Inscribing this rhetoric into the figure of Allenby, then, Fitzgerald makes his fictional football captain not just a Big Man on Campus, but the supposed flawless instance of a biological sport.

In this way, Amory's fascination with Allenby is not solely a product of Allenby's social persona but also his racial identity; Allenby is the Princeton embodiment of what many sportswriters were calling the White Hope. The phrase "White Hope" was initially coined as a nickname for Jim Jeffries, a boxer who came out of retirement to fight then-heavyweight champion Jack Johnson. Jeffries claimed that he was "going into this fight for the sole purpose of proving that a white man is better than a Negro" (Bederman 2). Hobey Baker, in being consistently contrasted with Jack Johnson, might be seen as a sort of natural inheritor of the "White Hope" label after Jeffries was trounced by Johnson, and Fitzgerald's portrayal of the whiteness of Allenby's platoon could be seen as a recognition of this. Amory's fascination with Allenby and desire to become like him physically (by playing football) and socially (by being a Big Man) is bound up not only in the aura of Allenby's athleticism but in the power of the whiteness as well. We've already seen how football, by claiming superiority on the grounds of an equitable competition on the gridiron, is able to reinforce the social system; football, as a physical game, also easily reinforces ideologies of social Darwinism. The logic works like this: 1) The ideal football player is strong and able-bodied, making him most likely to succeed. 2) Because the strong and able-bodied succeed in football, they must be the most qualified to occupy the elite social position granted to the football star. 3) If physical strength is of such paramount importance, so too must other physical features be important, not just for athletic success but also for the subsequent social success. 4) Ivy League football stars were, as evident with Hobey Baker, very often white and Nordic. 5) The white, Nordic figure must be the ideal figure of social elitism. This progression of "logic" would, in the minds of those writing the Princeton Freshman Handbook, speaking at graduation, or composing books about the moral value of football, provide a justification for claiming that white, socially elite figures are naturally more suited to the physical rigors of being in positions of power and have, in fact, earned their privilege. Fallacious, perhaps, but Fitzgerald exposes how football in the twentieth century provides just such an argument for those already in the positions of power. Given this sort of cultural thought, it becomes even clearer why football was so championed at Princeton.

NIGHT WALKING

The concept of social Darwinism is woven into the text by Fitzgerald in other ways and is subtly connected to the football subtext of Amory's initial glimpse of Allenby. As Burne Holiday instigates the insurrection in the Princeton eating clubs, he and Amory have a drawn-out conversation involving everything "from biology to organized religion" (*TSOP* 119). In fact, Amory and Burne have several subsequent conversations that consistently return to the efficacy of social Darwinism. They discuss "the matter of the bearing of physical attributes on a man's make-up," including physical strength and vigor (122). They also talk about "personal appearance," later clarified as "coloring" by Amory:

> We took the year-books for the last ten years and looked at the pictures of the senior council . . . only about thirty-five per cent of every class here are blonds, are really light—yet two-thirds of every senior council are light. (122)

This connection of Nordic, blond-haired appearance with social success is uniquely reminiscent of those blond locks of Hobey Baker. Even Burne reluctantly "admits" to the social power of the light-haired, light-skinned boy over the darker one, the text once more reinforcing the way that social class distinctions (whether student council or football captain), by being figured as racial distinctions, are impervious to penetration from those outside of the circle. It is no wonder that Fitzgerald, even at this young age disillusioned by his inability to crack the social hierarchy himself, paints Amory as having dark, auburn hair, in opposition to Fitzgerald's own physical resemblance to athletic and social stars such as Hobey Baker.

This is not to ignore the fact that Amory's language is also an expression of racial fear. The fact that racial language of physicality is superimposed upon conversation about social difference is crucial, considering the common American nationalist rhetoric of anti-immigration and racial suppression that was so prevalent during World War I and beyond. Amory, in one scene in the novel, exhibits such fear while taking a trip from Washington back to Princeton. Thoughts of World War I, the war that "rolled swiftly up the beach and washed the sands where Princeton played" (139), cause Amory to muse upon prevalent theories of national homogeneity:

> The berths across from him were occupied by stinking aliens—Greeks, he guessed, or Russians. He thought how much easier it would have been to fight as the Colonies fought, or as the Confederacy fought. And he did no sleeping that night, but listened to the aliens guffaw and snore while they filled the car with the heavy scent of latest America. (139)

Amory's thoughts, which take place as he is traveling back toward Princeton instead of away from it, demonstrate several things. First of all, they demonstrate the degree to which he truly does not understand the social composition of America. Amory seems resistant to the fact that there is a country outside of the walls of Princeton. Yet the novel's treatment of social Darwinism and xenophobia are crucial for understanding the way that football connects social hierarchy and racial fear. Amory's perception of the social stratification at Princeton is simultaneously bound up in the rhetoric of American nativism, the belief that America should be a land reserved solely for those capable (for physical and cultural reasons) of identifying themselves as "Americans." Walter Benn Michaels, in *Our America*, defines nativism as a belief system that "involved not only a reassertion of the distinction between American and un-American but a crucial redefinition of the terms in which it might be made" (2).

A Princeton-centric vision of America, that with which Amory has been indoctrinated, that which has been ingrained since his Freshman year, is an America of a glittering caste system and easily defined, immutable lines of social distinction. Princeton's America is an America of a handful of rich, white youth marching around singing football cheers. This is why a system such as Princeton goes to such great lengths to market football heroes and make the sport such a vocal factor in the rhetoric of superiority. As mentioned earlier, the football hero is the type of person Princeton desired to represent them because of the visible nature of the sport and the spectatorship surrounding it. More importantly, though, the football hero is *visually* the desirable figure to serve as a type of Princeton privilege and as an example of Hibben's "exemplary men" that reached prominence through "natural law." Analyzing this ideological position requires asking a vital question: Is Allenby's social status a product of the way he plays or the way he looks? He presumably had athletic talent, although it is never once portrayed in the novel. Generally speaking, football is a sport reliant upon physical prowess, but Allenby's characterization consistently avoids discussion of his playing abilities. Allenby is more prominently the end result of Walter Camp's promises about football's usefulness to the nation's young men; he's the figure that a nativist would hold up as the "prototypical" American. He is also a tool of ideological perpetuation; by initially offering social prestige to aspiring figures, promising them success like that observed in the pictures of Allenby (where his physical makeup trumps any sense of his talent), the Princeton freshman year indoctrinates students into a world where physical composition leads to delineation of haves and have-nots. Amory, due to the "haze of his own youth" (88), is deceived into thinking that Princeton Football as America is more advantageous than all the racial and ethnic diversity of "latest America."

Burne, admittedly, does not dispute the preponderance of lighter complexions among individuals with social prestige, and even compares the physical make-up of Princeton student council members to that of American presidents (123). However, Burne does not see biological difference as a cause of social distinction, but as a representation of it. That is, he sees it as the *result* of the social system of classification striving to advertise its "natural" place rather than the *cause* of the system. Burne in actuality strives to separate himself from such a system in much the same way he separates himself from the eating-club practices. He resigns from the student council and spends most of his time reading and walking: "walking at night was one of his favorite pursuits" (123). Burne picks up where his brother Kerry leaves off, providing the ideological voice opposing Princeton's way of doing things, hoping to get through to Amory and let him know that, for the nation, there is a better way than playing football to deal with the reality of physical and social difference in America. Burne's walking, a physical activity yet one differing from football in a variety of ways, is emblematic of his own attempts to conceive of an alternative to the society he has been bucking his entire Princeton career.

Burne soon invites Amory along on a walk as a sort of initiation into the problems of social Darwinism. Using very symbolic language, the text describes their nighttime walk and the significance Burne ascribes to it. "I hate the dark," Amory first objects (123). Such a statement, when following soon after his earlier conversation with Burne about "coloring" and its relation to social standing, can be read as yet another of Amory's assertions that he does not want to be associated with anything marginalized (for whatever reason). He does not want to be on the outside, on the fringes of a society, but at the center. His expression of a fear of the "dark" thus expresses his assumption that to be non-white is to be displaced, just as to be socially excluded is to be on the outside. Yet Burne encourages him to continue walking:

> "Any person with any imagination is bound to be afraid," said Burne earnestly. "And this very walking at night is one of the things I was afraid about. I'm going to tell you why I can walk anywhere now and not be afraid." (124)

Burne is assuming the role that Amory initially hoped Allenby would play, that of social guide. Burne's goal is to teach Amory to live in the "latest America," the America of difference, and he sees metaphoric ideas of light and dark as the best language with which to do so. He continues:

> Well, I began analyzing it—My imaginations persisted in sticking horrors into the dark—so I stuck my imagination into the dark instead and let it look out at me . . . it always makes everything all right to project yourself completely into another's place . . . one night I sat down and dozed off in there; then I knew I was through being afraid of the dark." (124)

Burne is, first and foremost, relying on the images of the "horrors" of the dark—that which is visibly undesirable, where race (being dark) is a horror that must be confronted.

But by speaking of racial difference, Burne is speaking, to a certain degree, of difference in total. One of the issues at the heart of racism is segregation, and, as Ann Douglas writes in *Terrible Honesty*, the leading practitioners of Social Darwinism, including sociologists, eugenicists, psychologists, and anthropologists, "explained that 'race' designated and included not just color but ethnicity, nationality, and, even by implication, class and language" (305). This has been especially true for discussions of national progress. A good deal of the rhetoric about the place sport held in American society emphasizes physical strength and prowess as the foundation for a strong national character. Theodore Roosevelt, in his 1898 essay "The Value of an Athletic Training," asserts that

> the great development and wide diffusion and practice of athletic exercises among our people during the last quarter of a century (this diffusion taking place precisely among those classes where the need of it was greatest) has been a very distinct advantage to our national type. (1236)

By utilizing the phrase "national type," Roosevelt implies a concept of a national race; his words carry a subtext that there are physical requirements for being American. Part of the emphasis on athletic training as an integral feature of national character is based on the fear of physical degeneration leading to loss of community—the weaker societies might fall prey to the stronger. Such a fear, expressed first as one of physicality, inevitably led to similar expressions of economic and social degeneration, demonstrated in Francis Walker's claim that what was once American economic and social superiority was being undermined by immigration (Higham 143). Because of such assumptions, proponents of social Darwinism, in expressing a fear of physical erosion and a fear of racial deterioration, were attempting to avert an eventual breakdown of class distinction as well.

"A RESTLESS GENERATION"

Amory's walk through the dark with Burne in *This Side of Paradise* necessarily precludes any discussion of football. In fact, that sport is so rarely referenced in relation to either of the Holiday brothers is a deliberate, marked absence. Football is what helps teach Amory at Princeton; the night walk with Burne is his education outside the walls. It is a recognition that the America on the other side of the ivy really *is not* homologous to the campus life, and the social system that Princeton is clinging to, that of rewarding privilege and freezing mobility would not work for the "latest America." Burne's theories of bridging racial difference intersect with the lessons in socialism that he and his brother Kerry had earlier tried to instill in Amory. While it would be simplistic to claim that race relations are all about class, such loci of identity are certainly bound up in each other. By inflecting Burne's class philosophies with the language and cultural rhetoric of race, the text reveals what football illuminates as the true failure of the social system at Princeton—the inability to get beyond self-centered social life and recognize that, in terms of social stratification, the privileged, gentrified student body cannot conceive of a life outside of the walls.

Fitzgerald never intended for *This Side of Paradise* to be a revolutionary tract on racial equality, nor did he mean for it to be read as a resounding endorsement of socialism. Amory's struggles within the conflicting voices of Princeton football and the Holiday brothers does not even suggest that there was a tenable solution to the class tension of early twentieth-century American life. What Fitzgerald ultimately does in the novel is expose the problems inherent in the exclusionary system that Princeton represents. Or, as he puts it in a letter to Edmund Wilson, the book "rather damns much of Princeton" (323). After Amory leaves school, and for a while forgets the ideologies expressed by Kerry and Burne, he literally drifts from place to place, never finding any more social satisfaction than he had at Princeton. But late in the novel, Amory recalls some of the arguments of the Holiday brothers—he remembers "the sense of security he had found with Burne" (246)—and attempts to explore the prospect of socialism as an alternative social system for the nation as a whole. Amory, without money and without a place to go, decides to walk from Manhattan back toward Princeton, metaphorically returning to the root of his early education. As he begins this journey, he is approached by two men offering him a job out "West . . . [because] the West is especially short of labor" (247). As they enter a conversation about the merits of capitalism, Amory suddenly claims that the American capitalist civilization is just "going round and round in a circle. That—is the great middle class!" (255). Amory invokes not just Kerry Holiday's ideology but his actual language, painting an image of a nation unable to progress socially but instead caught in a never-ending loop. Amory, experiencing a "loss of faith" and a "full realization of his disillusion" (245–46), sees that socialism is, if not a solution, perhaps his "only Panacea" (256). It is not a specific resolution to the tensions of social stratification, but a hope of a cure-all, some intangible promise that may not exist but certainly must be a better alternative than the system in which he was educated.

It is finally outside of Princeton's grounds—"Eight hours from Princeton" in the middle of "the frost-bitten country" (257)—where he is able to recognize that he can never be included in the echelons of privileged Princeton society. Amory connects this recognition inextricably with a much larger modern American alienation:

> My whole generation is restless. I'm sick of a system where the richest
> man gets the most beautiful girl if he wants her, where the artist without

an income has to sell his talents to a button manufacturer. . . . It seems to me I've been a fish out of water in too many outworn systems. I was probably one of the two dozen men in my class at college who got a decent education; still they'd let any well-tutored flathead play football and I was ineligible. (256)

In this passage, the text finally re-invokes the discussion of football and its role in helping Amory understand the problems in the social stratification Princeton practiced. Amory's speech to the two proponents of capitalism links the football-playing "flathead" to the two figures of the upper-class beside whom Fitzgerald continually felt inadequate and who continually represented the failure of the American Dream—the rich man getting the girl and the capitalist society that commodifies literature. What's more, the so-called flathead, the one being encouraged to succeed by the system, is "tutored" in the ways of success. Amory is referencing an earlier experience where he witnesses the "illiterate athlete" Langueduc being tutored in conic sections. Langueduc, "who would beat Yale this fall if only he could muster a poor fifty percent," is representative of all the "prominent athletes" at Princeton who, in order to preserve their eligibility, are coached through every answer (93). Amory, frustrated that someone possessing "six-foot-three of football material" is given not only targeted assistance but also tremendous leeway, identifies perhaps the biggest flaw in the social system at Princeton, where Langueduc's status of football star earns him preferential treatment while Amory is forced to eke out survival on his own.

By examining Amory's reference here to his memory of Langueduc, however, we also remember that Amory was never declared ineligible for football—he was injured. Yet he *was* declared academically ineligible to serve as editor of *The Princetonian* for failing his exams (exams coming on the heels of the Langueduc experience). This detail is significant as the reader learns more about the men with whom he's conversing. One of the pair asks Amory about his education. Mentioning Princeton, Amory is surprised to learn that this man is the father of Amory's old classmate, Jesse Ferrenby, a name connected to the entire episode with Langueduc and Amory's failed exams. The observant reader will remember that Ferrenby, one of Amory's particular friends, was also his major competition for the position of chief editor of *The Princetonian,* and got the position after Amory was denied it because of his grades. Amory's earlier remark thus takes on added meaning; Amory was never declared ineligible to play football but to write for the paper, yet the two endeavors become conflated in his mind. Amory recognizes that ineligibility for the *Princetonian* is not as tragic as ineligibility for football, and so exclusion along athletic lines becomes his language for talking about exclusions as a whole. Football is status at Princeton, and "ineligibility," or the removal of what Amory saw as the only sign of his social status, can only be codified in athletic terms.

Metaphorically, then, Jesse Ferrenby, who Amory saw "wearing a hungry look and watching him eagerly" when he received notification of his failing grades (95), is likewise one of the "flatheads" who play football. He is the product of the system in which Amory could never compete. Moreover Ferrenby, who died with glory in World War I,[9] is "the man who in college had borne off the crown that he had aspired to" (257). He is the epitome of the failure of the culture, a representation of the realization that at Princeton they were all "little boys," working for the spot, the position, the trophy, or the ribbon. Amory identifies Princeton football as the most specific example of the many systems which make his "whole generation" restless, and subsequently even more firmly associates the flaws of the Princeton system with the flaws of the American system. Football is not a straw man for Amory, but a very tangible representation of where the nation is going wrong. Significantly, Amory readily admits to the men with whom he's conversing that he does not necessarily believe that socialism is the answer, either. Amory knows that his words are just ideas. Amory is merely arguing for any type of change, something different from the system in which he has been brought up, something that can "struggle against tradition" (256)[10].

In the novel's final image, Amory stands at night, observing the University that has had such power over his way of thinking for so long, and hears the bells echoing through the spires. The image is hauntingly reminiscent of Amory's first night at Princeton, listening to Allenby's song as he and the football phalanx marched through the campus. Yet all of Amory's Romantic visions have been shattered as a result of the past few years of his life. He muses upon the "new generation" at the school, the youth just encountering the indoctrination and marketing of the social hierarchy, and knows that though they are "still fed romantically on the mistakes and half-forgotten dreams" of those coming before them, they will soon discover themselves "grown up to find all Gods dead, all wars fought, all faiths in man shaken" (260).

At its heart, *This Side of Paradise*'s use of football is a recognition that modern American life is inextricably caught in a game of social tension—a social contest between the elite, privileged status of the Allenbys and the radical socialism of the Holiday brothers. And football is not merely the language through which this struggle is evident, but also the cultural institution through which the struggle is played out. The story that Princetonian football puts forth about social standing, division, and mobility (or lack thereof), as Fitzgerald's "intense and dramatic spectacle" that symbolizes the failure of the culture within the walls of Princeton, was faulty from the start. In other words, those striving to impose their own class-based values upon football perpetuated the narratives of the game friendly to their ideologies. Fifteen years later, in the nostalgic essay "Sleeping and Waking," Fitzgerald would articulate about football what he had already illustrated in *This Side of Paradise:* because football is so bound up in class tensions, Romantic notions of athleticism lead only to cultural failure rather than to personal success— "It's no use—I have used that dream of a defeated dream to induce sleep for almost twenty years, but it has worn thin at last" (66). Worn thin not just for himself, but for the nation, for his generation "try[ing], at least, to displace old cants with new ones" (*TSOP* 256).

Chapter Three
"Idol of the Whole Body of Young Men": Football, Heroes, and the Performance of Social Status

Amory Blaine was not Fitzgerald's first attempt at examining the question of how football functions in a culture—nor would he be the last. Much of Fitzgerald's "material," as he put it, was utilized in short fiction written for both the "slick" mass-market periodicals (notably *The Saturday Evening Post* and *Esquire*) as well as for literary magazines (such as H.L. Mencken's *The Smart Set*). The game of football (most often as played at the college level) makes an appearance in more than two dozen of these stories. More significantly, football plays a major narrative role in at least eight.

A common refrain in current Fitzgerald scholarship is to look at his short stories as a "use of the popular magazines as a workshop for his novels, demonstrating as it does his growing awareness of the fact that he can experiment with ideas in his stories that will be developed and refined later in longer works" (Mangum 67). This is a valid assessment of some of his well-known and well-studied stories.[1] But when it comes to some of the lesser known stories, including those that make football a primary feature of plot and setting, it's difficult to locate any *direct* connections in terms of character, plot detail, or imagery between Fitzgerald's football-oriented short fiction and his novels. He never develops prototypes of Amory Blaine in his early short fiction nor reworks such a persona in later stories, nor does he create embryonic versions of other characters that would appear in his novels, even when football is designed to be a major part of the characterization of such figures.[2] Given that the football stories don't neatly fit into Mangum's model, it would be difficult, and indeed not very fruitful, to assume that they exist solely as the remnants of Fitzgerald's literary workshops that prepared him for more serious writing. These short stories are, instead, their own entities, interacting with different aspects of the American cultural scene. As Jackson R. Bryer writes, Fitzgerald's stories "should not be read merely or even primarily for what they can tell us about Fitzgerald's life or about his novels and better-known stories . . . [these] stories are in and of themselves deserving of our scrutiny" (6). Certainly, as cultural texts, Fitzgerald's football stories deserve to be scrutinized for the things they reveal about the role of football during the early twentieth century.

Interestingly, in *This Side of Paradise* there was no portrayal of real football action—that is, the reader never sees a character actually engaged in playing the game. Instead, all the attention is given to football heroes or those aspiring to become like them as they live their lives off the field. Football, as an actual sport, is in certain ways absent from the novel while its traces become the prominent factor in exploring the complexities of the social relationships between heroes, worshippers, and the ideological figures controlling both. In Fitzgerald's world of short fiction, however, we very often find visual descriptions of the physical, athletic action of football, sometimes incessantly so; the plot of the individual texts detail narratives of football players who set themselves apart from the spectators (whether we're talking about direct observers of an individual game or the fans who simply follow the athletic careers of the "heroes") *on* the field as well as off. Because of this, Fitzgerald's stories depicting football action are extremely intriguing in their use of terms such as "spectacle," "drama," and "play," word choices which link directly to concepts of performance. These stories also often contain extended metaphors or analogies between the action of the football game and theatrical settings, Hollywood personae, and a sense of audience-oriented, constructed rehearsing. As Fitzgerald narratively explores the connection between the game of football and some of these settings, his football stories describe the physical action of football and its consequences not as an athletic competition, but as a staged show, a play in which actors assume roles that bring them romantic and monetary accolades.

When I say that Fitzgerald explores the degree to which those playing football were participating in a performance, I am specifically interested in aspects of performance having to do with a public construction of social communication. Erving Goffman writes that

> A "performance" may be defined as all the activity of a given participant on a given occasion which serves to influence in any way any of the other participants. Taking a particular participant and his performance as a basic point of reference, we may refer to those who contribute to the other performances as the audience, observers, or co-participants. (15)

According to Goffman's definition, performance behaviors are in many ways communicative actions, building upon the relationship between the figures involved in the action of a performance and those involved in the watching of it. In this way, performance is an interactive expression that relies upon social relationships and establishes new (or expands upon already existing) social roles and lines of social hierarchy.

Goffman continues his definition of performance as an inherently social behavior by focusing on the idea that performance is also an inherently recursive action:

> Defining "social role" as the enactment of rights and duties attached to a given status, we can say that a social role will involve one or more parts and that each of these different parts may be presented by the performer on a series of occasions to the same kinds of audiences or to an audience of the same persons. (16)

In other words, to be called a performance, an action must be repetitive in nature. Generally, we think of this in terms of rehearsal and reenactment of a previously determined pattern (such as a script), and this will certainly be part of Fitzgerald's understanding of football as performance. But as Richard Schechner points out, the repetition necessary in performance doesn't necessarily require exact duplication of actions; instead, he calls performance the enacting of "twice-behaved behaviors," a concept which postulates that specific, small-scale behaviors are often rehearsed to the point that, even though specific events or interactions happening for the first time may not be replications of previous occurrences, they are still made up of a series of scripted actions (33). In effect, this concept of twice-behaved behaviors relies upon familiar stories—those related to concepts of history, genealogy, or ritual—to communicate social behaviors that are both unique as well as repetitive.

When examining the connections between football and performance in Fitzgerald's short stories, it is this idea of twice-behaved behaviors that forms the building blocks of Fitzgerald's description of football action and characterization of football players and fans. Admittedly, in arguing that Fitzgerald sees football as a behavior of social performance, this doesn't necessarily mean I view him as portraying the game as unreal or fraudulent. Nor do I attribute a sense of deception to the performance behaviors we read in Fitzgerald's football stories. Instead I focus on the constructed nature of performance—how, on the part of the fans and the players, the games they constantly take part in or watch structure stories of social status. Performance sets the behavior of its agents apart from unique, self-contained occurrences and creates stories which then guide their interactions away from the playing field.

Thirty years after Fitzgerald's writing, Edwin Cady looked at football and formulated a structured, coherent outlook of the game that made concrete some of the ideas which Fitzgerald was so clearly concerned about in terms of the relationship between football and performance. In 1978, Cady published a scholarly analysis of the relationship between college football and media through the first three quarters of the twentieth century. Calling football the "Big Game," Cady first and foremost emphasizes the notion that the history of football is a history of a spectacle. By labeling football with the word "Big," his analysis looks at the larger structures at work in the interplay between athletes playing football and fans watching it. Cady's narrative of football's history emphasizes communication between fans and players and sees the relationship as one that creates a sphere of social interaction that was larger than that taking place in the individual game on the field (between players, for example).

Specifically, when Cady talks about the story of "the Big Game" he focuses on the ways in which the players' performance influences the fans who have gathered to watch. He writes,

> In connection with [the Big Game] a number of different games go on simultaneously, inside the stadium and out. Though all focus on and take symbolic cues from the game the athletes play, each plays to its own ends. (62–63)

Within this public sphere, those watching notice the "symbolic cues" of the football game, in essence for their own subsequent performances. Though Cady does see this sort of social interaction *originating* with the performance on the field, it is centered most fully on the crowd. According to Cady's logic, the existence of football performance within a public sphere, "public beyond all previous imagining" (62), as he puts it, allows the crowd to, through simultaneously witnessing the game on the field, participate in a larger game—that of the historical narrative of football-as-social interaction. "Everything starts . . . from 'givens' provided by the past. . . . The game itself, as a pattern of culture and form of art, as a set of skills, conventions, and rules, comes to the field or floor and the stands as a given" (63). Football performance, as a social behavior fundamentally situated within the probing eyes of spectators, relies upon the patterns which the players, coaches, and fans are continually repeating through this form of social interaction.

Cady also claims that the fans hold more power in the relationship between the crowd and the player. In other words, the spectators can better determine how the actions occurring on a football field lead to off the field social status or honor. Cady uses his argument to demonstrate how the word "game" redefines itself through performance, conceptually sliding from a word that labels sporting activity to a word that provides a sense of playful social interaction. The crowd rewards the players for their actions, but only according to how well they "play" and how well they match up to the audience's expectations. And, according to Cady's argument, this interchange between fan and athletic performer is itself a much more powerful level of game or play. The performance of a football game sets the stage for a larger, social performance that creates the formation of status-groups and recreates rituals of social relationship.

THE "DRAMATIC ESSENCE" OF FOOTBALL

The last chapter discussed how Fitzgerald's Allenby, because of his status and popularity, found his place at the top of a social hierarchy dependent upon the fans who observed and idolized him; or, in the words of George Santayana in an essay entitled "Philosophy on the Bleachers," athletic events comprising the Big Game are "public spectacles in which . . . spectators are indispensable, since without them, the victory, which should be the only reward, would lose half its power" (qtd. in Cady 33). Santayana thus reinforces the concept of performance as a public, social communication. He also theorizes as to *how* the performance behaviors of football maps out a model of social hierarchy. He argues that football is a "physical drama" which "displays the dramatic essence of physical conflict" yet is simultaneously the foundation for an idea of "vicarious interest" (33). Football is a physical sport that requires the participation of real bodies as well as genuine skill to perform in an effective manner. Yet the game of football takes place in a public space, one constructed specifically for the purpose of playing a game. Fans packing themselves into a stadium to watch a football game participate in a structural replay of similar activities that have already taken place numerous times. Thus the performance develops a sort of ritual nature, a ritual built on vicarious participation and identification.

The actions of a football game are, in this way, an amalgam of natural and artificial action. For Santayana, it is this paradox in the ritualistic nature which creates the strong sense of sport as a communicative performance, leading him to conclude that the spectators invest their time, energy, and devotion in the game because it is a situation that allows for demonstrations of not only physical conflict but also the "virtues and fundamental gifts of man" (33). This assumption positions football play as a re-enactment of social play in which more advanced skill is a representation of "virtues"; such a play then connects to the narrative that sees football as a virtue-building sport and, subsequently, uses concepts of "virtue" and "refinement" to build social models of hierarchy and inclusion/exclusion. In other words, Cady's theory that football is a performance in front of the fans helps to explain the structures underlying the cultural icons such as the "Big Man on Campus" that were so much a part of class formations of the late nineteenth and early twentieth centuries.

Fitzgerald's football stories seem to anticipate Cady's theories, focusing on the spectacle of football and its structures of performance behavior and social communication more than on its personalities. Significantly, this connection between football and performance approaches the question of what football has to do with American social class from a different perspective than the previous chapter. While both seek to investigate the relationship between spectator and fan as a way to understand better the hierarchical social systems and their implications, Amory Blaine's football story participates in a very specific cultural conversation with Walter Camp, Theodore Roosevelt, and the ideological hierarchy of authority and schools such as Princeton. Though fictional, *This Side of Paradise* is concerned with *historical* stories and tangible American cultural objects, seeking to know what football can do in Fitzgerald's Princeton and/or his America. To put it another way, *This Side of Paradise* is engaged in a cultural conversation with things that were said or written by real people. The short stories, however, have a different relationship to past narratives in that Fitzgerald's characters in short fiction are more intriguingly juxtaposed with other *fictional* characters rather than with historical figures. It is as if the short stories are Fitzgerald's attempt to respond to questions that had been asked by the heritage of football stories preceding his writing. In a sense, I am locating Fitzgerald's football stories in a sort of literary football history, providing a more complex look at the role the football hero plays in society and what the relationship between players and fans means for social interaction.

To be more concrete when I use a phrase such as "authors and their fictional characters," in this chapter I will juxtapose Fitzgerald's short football fiction against stories such as those of fictional Yale football star, Frank Merriwell. This approach makes sense partially because of the significant connection between the mass-market audience for which the authors both wrote. More noteworthy, however, is the nature of the codes and practices of the football hero story; in some ways football for Fitzgerald is a performance in a double sense, as he both represented football as a "twice-behaved behavior" but also as he "performed" the act of writing his football stories as a conventionalized narrative in relation to precursor fictions.

The Frank Merriwell stories, written for the pulp fiction magazine *Tip Top Weekly* between 1896 and 1913,[3] follow the title character from his days at the imaginary prep school Fardale Academy through his college career at Yale. Gilbert Patten, writing under the pen name of Burt L. Standish, composed these stories about Frank and his various activities on a weekly basis, keeping his reading public apprised of the latest imaginary escapades of his hero. Patten's Merriwell narratives were not merely tales of youthful adventure and decisive action, but also, in the tradition of Horatio Alger, stories with didactic plots of moral choice. Frank often had Alger-like "adventures" in outdoor settings, in social situations, in schoolroom escapades, or even in common dime-novel stock plots of detective work or cowboy fantasies; however, Patten's depiction of Frank and his world located heroism in a different environment from that which Alger or other mass-market writers had explored. Frank Merriwell's adventures centered most fully around his athleticism, and the action of these narratives continually climaxed with his sporting contests and with the relationship that his fictional social standing bore to his ability to score the winning run or make a game-saving tackle.

Because I emphasize this sort of literary conversation between Fitzgerald and Gilbert Patten (or perhaps it could be phrased a literary descendancy), it is important to sketch out the way in which the Frank Merriwell stories deal with performance, status, and the cultural narratives of football. The Merriwell series is a particular instance of what Ralph D. Gardner calls "hero fiction" (103). This fiction, pioneered by Alger's *Tattered Tom* and *Ragged Dick,* produces characters supposedly embodying qualities of persistence, endurance, and moral strength, qualities which, according to the logic of hero fiction narratives, give the characters their success as well as their popularity. The "heroes" of hero fiction were composed to be idol-like figures for the juvenile audiences reading the dime novels and pulp magazines[4] in which hero fiction appeared. Particular pulp magazines were usually devoted to a particular kind of hero fiction—adventure stories, detective stories, westerns, science fiction, etc. Frank Merriwell was one of the first, and was certainly the most popular, of hero fiction characters whose fame and fortune went hand in hand with his athletic abilities.

Though the Merriwell stories were not serialized novels, after the run of the series many stories were collected together and bound in paperback as if they were novels. This was possible because from story to story, though the setting or the conflict might change, thematically each story was a variation on a single theme: Frank's achievements and his status as school leader were directly related to his status as a sport star. In other words, the stories were very overt in promulgating the American story of sport—that the player with the greater abilities rises to the top of the social ladder. The Merriwell stories use Frank's athleticism to portray fictionally such themes as acquiring social success through athleticism, and in fact often sound like testimonials to Roosevelt's strenuous life or Walter Camp's theories of football being able to convert a callow youth into a "successful man." In "Frank Merriwell at Yale," for example, Frank muses upon the prospects of an athlete at Yale:

> The democratic spirit at Yale came mainly from athletics, as Frank soon discovered. Every class had half a dozen teams—tennis, baseball, football, the crew and so on. Everybody, even the "greasy" grinds, seemed interested in something, and so one or more of these organizations had some sort of a claim on everybody. . . . In athletics strength and skill win, regardless of money or family; so it happened that the poorest man in the university stood a show of becoming the lion and idol of the whole body of young men. (259–260)

Frank was portrayed as both the epitome of "strength and skill," serving, throughout the years, as captain of the football, baseball, and crew teams. More significantly, Frank was consistently the embodiment of "the idol of the whole body of young men" spoken about in the above passage. He was the figure to be admired, to be worshipped; he was the person at the center of social interaction. These two facts go hand in hand according to Patten's logic. Labeling the playing of football as a social act, one based in performance, sets the stage for treating the figures of strength and skill on the gridiron as "idols."

Of course, the phrase "the idol of the whole body of young men" is not just a description of how Patten portrayed the relationship between Frank and his fictional Yale classmates, but is also an astute statement of what the character of Frank Merriwell meant to young boys in America reading his adventures week after week. Frank's sporting adventures were exciting enough and ubiquitous enough to make him the idol of America's youth, young boys who dreamed of days when they, too, could win the game on the final play and walk off the field with their names echoing throughout the crowd. Reading a Frank Merriwell story was a ritualistic experience; he was worshipped by his audience of young boys week after week, in large part because the plot details of his stories changed little and often recombined smaller parts of previous plots. Interestingly enough, Patten himself had little knowledge of American college life (Messenger 167). But Patten's (lack of) experience with college is not what made the Merriwell series sell so well; his experience with the world of pulp fiction was. Specifically, it is the repetition and patterns in Patten's narrative structures that are much more important in understanding what the Merriwell stories offered. The most common narrative "rituals"— the most frequently reproduced performances—were the stock tales replete with no competent adults, a tense conflict arising early on between Frank and a schoolmate villain, and some last-minute heroics to win the game. In each case, the re-enactments of these plots all underscore a very didactic message: Frank Merriwell, through the performance of a given story, teaches a very visible and easily acceptable path to social recognition. In essence, Patten formulates a football narrative which, to the readers of his fiction, would act rhetorically in terms of persuading the young boys that this narrative was the way to find social prestige or position.

As was the case with Fitzgerald's Allenby, Patten's Merriwell saw success that was not merely athletic. He was without fail the quintessence of "proper," approved social behavior, and it is this fact that cemented his popularity even more among those reading his stories. Frank was the model citizen, the gentleman that everyone in the stories rallied around. "'I owe it all to Merriwell,'" exclaims Bart Hodge in one Merriwell tale, and then goes on to elaborate:

> He taught me, gentlemen, that a man can be a man without always carrying a chip on his shoulder. He taught me that a man can preserve his dignity without compelling every weaker man to bow to him in humbleness. But I know that he can fight when pushed to it. ("Tested")

As portrayed in such stories, Merriwell has "dignity" and honor, and teaches this through means other than formal instruction. His life on the gridiron and his life off of it parallel each other in terms of "virtue" and "moral," his off-field behavior becoming yet another level of performance that re-enacts his football or baseball behaviors. In essence, the stories demonstrate that there is no "original" behavior, but that Frank's social life is also a ritual, replayed week after week just as his athletic heroics are.

The Merriwell stories also laid out a pattern for what type of social hierarchy developed through the ritual performances that took place on the gridiron. As such a heroic figure, Frank was the one always placed in positions of responsibility (both formally and informally) in the fictional Yale microcosm. Through Frank's position, Patten was able to overtly connect athletics to the "democratic spirit" mentioned above. This phrase "democratic spirit" is an earlier version of the narrative of meritocracy in which Fitzgerald's Amory

Blaine was absorbed. Frank Merriwell's popularity reinforced a belief that lines of social position were developed through ability rather than preconceived notions of privilege or elitism. Merriwell consistently spouted rhetoric of egalitarian opportunity and the possibilities of social mobility. For example,

> In the course of time Frank came to believe that the old spirit was still powerful at Yale. There were a limited number of young gentlemen who plainly considered themselves superior beings, and who positively refused to make acquaintances outside a certain limit; but those men held no positions in athletics, were seldom of prominence in the societies, and were regarded as cads by the men most worth knowing. They were to be pitied, not envied.
>
> At Yale the old democratic spirit still prevailed. The young men were drawn from different social conditions, and in their homes they kept to their own set; but they seemed to leave this aside, and they mingled and submerged their natural differences under that one broad generalization, "the Yale man." (258–59)

"The Yale man," just an alternate title for Walter Camp's model citizen football player (or perhaps we can say that Camp's model citizen is a re-enactment of Patten's Yale man), was Gilbert Patten's attempt to define the prototypical American. For Patten, the image of a social hodgepodge, a mass of people being "drawn from different social positions," goes hand in hand with class mobility and encouragement of social equality. Or, as he later puts it,

> Merriwell was to find that this extended even to their social life, their dances, their secret societies, where all who showed themselves to have the proper dispositions and qualifications were admitted without distinction of previous condition or rank in their own homes. . . . (259)

Of course, this type of egalitarianism is as illusionary as the product of Roosevelt's strenuous life, primarily because of the ironic emphasis on "proper dispositions and qualifications" despite the supposed abandonment of "rank" or class as a hierarchical formative power.

However, the paradox in the Merriwell formula, a paradox which Fitzgerald would find both fascinating and vexing, is in this consistent claim of merit-based success. Frank Merriwell, though claiming that the "democratic spirit" as exemplified through athletics would allow all to be "admitted without distinction of previous condition," is in fact a reinforcement of social distinction, in that he contradicts his own claims of egalitarianism among his society's youth. That is, Merriwell was depicted as a super-hero among boys; his athletic ability—his "strength and skill"—was a literary substitute for more common status-granting factors such as money or family. The fact that athleticism is a substitute for economic privilege is vital, given the discussions in the previous chapter about spectatorship, emulation, and social evolution. The physicality of football could be used to lend more credence to a sense of "natural" (as in biological) privilege than economic factors and could also encourage more of a desire to "be like the football star." But in the case of the Frank Merriwell stories, their being pulp fiction adds a new factor to the portrayal.

Michael Oriard, in discussing the spectacle of football as a cultural text, is quick to avoid totalizing his arguments by claiming that football shows "real people performing real acts" (9). The ritualistic performances of football players and the fans that watch them result in injuries that are real and bodies that are left in pain. The violence of the sport that Walter Camp tried so hard to veil was the "reality" on the playing field. But in the ink of Patten's pulp magazines, the performance was not real in the sense of being a historical record. In other words, Patten's fictional portrayal of the sport didn't accurately represent the physical brutality of the game. Patten's fictions are constructed, cultural texts which supersede the physical bodies playing the game. Merriwell, as an imagined character reincarnated over 900 times, is a rhetorical argument for the American narrative of sport as an allegory for class mobility. The fact that Patten's demonstrations of football and social performance belie their own fictional nature gave Fitzgerald something to respond to; it allowed him to interrogate this argument and find complexities in the allegorical story of athletic-based meritocracy that Gilbert Patten's Merriwell never exposed.

PULP HEROES AT THE TOP

Much is made of Fitzgerald's statements about his supposed disgust over having to write short stories for weekly or monthly periodicals. Perhaps the most oft-quoted line is in Fitzgerald's letter to Ernest Hemingway in which he stated that "The *Post* now pays the old whore $4000 a screw" (*Life* 169), thus comparing his literary endeavors to sexual power and his reliance on weekly short stories as a prostitution of his talent. But in the case of the football stories, the fact that Fitzgerald regarded them as mere commodities created to satisfy an audience and pay down debts paradoxically reinforces what Fitzgerald saw in football through writing for such periodicals. As Fitzgerald perceived it, mass-market publications were themselves a behavior of performance, in many ways because of the emphasis of the slicks on distribution—a periodical's form of communication—over content. In other words, the mass-market periodical was a medium highly self-conscious of the fact that it was a constructed object created for the pleasure of an audience. Publishing in the mass-market periodicals allowed Fitzgerald to place himself on stage to act out a part through his weekly or monthly characters. Patten, too, saw himself as a performer, in that his role was to create a show before the spectatorship of readers that would be foolproof in its ability to entertain. "To Patten," writes Messenger, the mass-market periodicals "were an amusement business in which it was his task to keep abreast of public taste and to write to meet that preference" (166). The description and short analysis of the Merriwell series which I presented earlier is, to utilize the language of performance, a script of sorts; this "script" made the Frank Merriwell stories a major contributor to, as Messenger notes, *Tip Top Weekly* sales of 500,000 copies per week at the height of its popularity. Fitzgerald, born in 1896, would have been the target age as a young boy for the Frank Merriwell series, and undoubtedly experienced what Christian Messenger calls the "dreams of adult authority," a system of youthful achievement made possible through such "escapist fiction" as Patten's stories (167). Most importantly, Patten's Frank Merriwell was a prototype, a constructed celebrity who inspired "boys by the thousands [to begin] to envision careers at Yale" (171)—or, in Fitzgerald's case, Princeton.

As mentioned earlier, Fitzgerald's attention to football in the short stories differs from his novels in that characters in the short fiction actually engage in playing football, and the descriptions of the game action play crucial roles in the narrative progression. In doing so, these stories follow a model that Patten established for the football story in which the main character is a hero. "Hero" is an intriguing word, one that Messenger applies to Fitzgerald's fictional characters and that hearkens back to the notion of "hero fiction" that made up so much of the pulp magazines and dime novels. Merriwell's heroic nature implies that his athletic actions could be described as a triumphant rescue, an engaging victory for his team snatched from the threat of defeat. Messenger describes Fitzgerald's attention to the hero figure by stating that the "range of roles for the School Sports Hero reveals [Fitzgerald's] great ability to infuse life into a stereotypical figure and provide it with a complex series of associations" (180). Messenger's observation is an astute one and particularly applicable to placing Fitzgerald's football heroes in dialogue with Frank Merriwell. Patten had been content with a simplistic, unchanging version of the hero, and the stories as a whole never doubt the efficacy of the assumption that a hero earns social prestige through greater skill or strength or through achieving something unusual. In other words, Patten portrays Merriwell's athletic accomplishments as a model of justification for privilege, seeing social status as a "natural" phenomenon and thus deserved. In this model of football-as-spectacle, when the fans see a great play or demonstration of strength they make an idol of the athlete by making him the center of their particular status group.

Consider a climactic scene in a Merriwell story about a Harvard-Yale game:

> Frank felt himself clutched, but he refused to be dragged down. He felt hands clinging to him, and, with all the fierceness he could summon, he strove to break away and go on. His lips were covered with a bloody foam, and there was a frightful glare in his eyes. He strained and strove to get a little farther, and actually dragged Hollender along the ground til [sic] he broke the fellow's hold. Then he reeled across Harvard's line and fell. ("Fun")

Merriwell's performance is a physical, gritty, violent image. Yet the violence actually underscores the way his actions allow him to interact with his fans, both the fictional ones watching his game and the real ones reading about it. Merriwell, as he exists within the bounds of the pulp page, behaves in such a way as to center the prestige on himself; he has both literal as well as figurative mass appeal. Moreover, in the next installment of the series, Merriwell has absolutely no scars, no wounds, no signs that a game had been played out in the ink of the previous week. Merriwell never actually gets hurt amidst all the violence portrayed in the pages of his stories. His strength, both physical and moral, seems limitless, and his body impervious to injury or pain. The mass appeal of the hero figure, combined with the constructed fiction of his actions, creates the social idol that garners social status and encourages ritualistic "worship." Though, as mentioned earlier, those in the position of "crowd" are the ultimate source of social power or prestige, the paradox is that the social hierarchies they control end up dictated by those they make idols out of. Merriwell always lives up to his role, and with the focus on such images of perseverance, endurance, strength, and courage Patten used Merriwell's performances as didactic tools. Patten reinforces the claim that Merriwell completely deserved the subsequent social accolades which he received from those who had witnessed his feat. In other words, the performance behaviors of being a football hero "earn" him the role of social idol. His week-to-week athletic performances are always subsumed within the larger moral tale that justifies social stratification.

Of course, while the social mores that dictate the formation of status groups out of athletic success are part of a culturally powerful narrative, the fictional framework in which Merriwell's feats were featured stages his actions just as a football stadium might, putting readers in the place of fans. Working with the assumption that the same holds true for the heroes of Fitzgerald's football fiction (although they are all, as we will see, very intentionally diametrically opposed to Merriwell in terms of skill as well as status), I suggest that Fitzgerald utilizes football in his short stories to interrogate the claims Patten makes about football and social status. Specifically, Fitzgerald sees a necessity in understanding better the degree to which Patten's didactic narrative plays itself out once freed from the ritual re-enactments of the Merriwell tales. Fitzgerald recognizes that being a successful football player necessitates engaging in performative behavior, and explores the ways in which the crowd both controls the creation of their idols while simultaneously relinquishes its social power to these idolized creations. In some ways, Fitzgerald finds himself torn, struggling to cast a shadow of doubt on the efficacy of Merriwell's endorsement of a strenuous life while also reluctant to release the Romantic notion of football as a path to becoming a social idol; consequently, he uses his short fiction to probe the football hero in much the same way as he probed the "Big Man" in *This Side of Paradise.*

Notably, the figure of the Big Man does differ somewhat from the hero figure; where the social standing of the Big Man figure is based in narratives of social "aura" more than any actual athletic success, the hero presumably demonstrates the skill and strength which the crowd demands. In other words, whereas the "source texts" of the Big Man's social power are the images, stories, and casual conversations about him, the text for the hero is that which directly interacts with the spectators—the game performance. And it is this distinction between the "Big Man" and the "Hero" which allows for an exploration of the football short fiction through the lens of performance and status. Ultimately in his football stories, Fitzgerald reveals that while playing football may have the power to allow for heroes to move to the center of a social status-group, such a phenomenon is not due to individual accomplishments or abilities but instead relies inherently upon a construction. The heroes lose their identity within the spectacle of football, as their actions, caught up in the performance, cling to a problematic narrative of earning status through sport-based meritocracy.

TELLING ABOUT IT: FITZGERALD'S FIRST FOOTBALL FICTION

While a student at the Newman School, Fitzgerald, playing for the school football team, embarrassed himself by dropping a pass he could have easily caught—quite an un-Merriwellian moment. He later penned a poem entitled "Football," which on one level might be seen as a wish-fulfillment reversal of his failure. More intriguing than the biographical or psychological connections, however, are the narrative connections, specifically the narrative created as Fitzgerald retells this experience late in life in his essay "Author's House":

> [The poem] made me as big a hit with my father as if I had become a football hero. So when I went home that Christmas vacation it was in my mind that if you weren't able to function in action you might at least be able to tell about it, because you felt the same intensity. . . . (40)

In this passage, Fitzgerald constructs an analogy between demonstrable physical skill and verbal skill—what he calls "telling about it." Fitzgerald uses the writing of literature as his metaphor in order to tap into the image of a writer as a public figure who composes directly for an audience, much as a football hero plays the game directly for a stadium full of fans. In theorizing that "telling about it" garners as much prestige in his father's eyes as winning the game might, Fitzgerald is implicitly arguing two points—1) a recognition of the relationship between successful athletic performance and social power, and 2) a recognition of the relationship between *appearing* to have athletic success and social power.[5] Thus he's giving his readers a key to reading football in his short stories, putting forth the notion that "real" strength and skill, while certainly present in football heroes, aren't as important in winning over the crowd as long as the fans are convinced of your prowess.

Reading his stories with the lens that his football heroes are "telling about it" demonstrates the response that his stories give to Patten and Merriwell; Fitzgerald offers complexities that Patten never explored. While Patten's Frank Merriwell stories attempted to argue that social prestige is within the reach of anyone, the unstated argument throughout the series was just the opposite, that physical superiority is a justification for social privilege. Frank Merriwell wasn't a "fake," in that he did have the strength and skill to be a successful football player; yet Fitzgerald, by "telling about it" in his football stories, gives portraits of characters who *don't* possess Merriwell's physical abilities yet still secure the same social status from the crowd by virtue of their masterful performances. Fitzgerald thus places the upper class in a tenuous position. Fitzgerald's use of football playing argues that if those idols who have athletic success have social power, yet that social power, dependent upon spectator adulation, doesn't have the basis in physical ability, then perhaps the system of social hierarchy which creates such idols is as much a fantasy as the constructions of football performance. Or at least, considering that the ability to perform is still a "skill," social hierarchy depends upon something other than natural talent.

Fitzgerald first recognized at least a trace of the performative nature of the game of football and the relationship that a fine "acting" athlete has with the fans observing him early in his literary career, when football as a socially-formative activity was a very prominent reality in his schoolboy life. During his "apprenticeship," [6] as he came to accept his own inabilities to succeed physically on the gridiron, he experimented with some early forms of "telling about it" to construct an idol in embryo. The result was the wishful, athletic fantasy of "Reade, Substitute Right Half." Critically, this piece of apprentice work has been dealt with primarily on biographical terms, but as a literary text it has yet to be deeply explored. The only brief analytical discussion has been by John Kuehl, who described it as "not overplotted and so [it] does not run the concomitant risks of melodrama and implausibility" (28). While this may be true, the language and descriptions in the text move beyond Kuehl's commentary; the story casts football as a spectacular, theatrical show and the athletes as gifted, but also scripted, actors, albeit in rudimentary, nascent traces.

As the story begins, readers enter the narrative as a "slogan" echoes through the crowd, "Hold! Hold! Hold!" (31). Following this initial cheer, the plot quickly shifts to the "battered, crimson warriors [*sic*]." Yet the importance of the chanting crowd as the opening frame emphasizes the province of the game as a spectacle before presenting it in metaphorics of a military engagement; in this way, the juxtaposition of these two images—the crowd and the football players represented through symbols of violent battle—set the stage as one of a performance of social communication. The fans themselves expect to see strength and skill, which they do, but only after the same group of spectators, in Fitzgerald's logic, are themselves privileged over those images of strength and skill. Given that the initial voice is that of the audience, the action as Fitzgerald describes it can thus be assessed as presented specifically for this mass of people surrounding the game. The story uses the crowd as a framework, making the narrative less one of football action and more one of sociability. Or, to be more precise, physical action only holds significance within the bounds of the crowd, creating a relationship much more dependent than usually admitted about athletic stars. The "crimson warriors" are, through the war imagery, hero figures, but their heroic status is created by their ability to respond to the "Hold! Hold! Hold!" of the crowd.

Following these opening lines, Fitzgerald introduces his readership to the main character, small-bodied Reade, who has perpetually sat on the bench until, at the moment of this story, he is called to replace a player who has succumbed to injury. Reade's stature when compared to the other "crimson warriors," as well as his status as a benchwarming backup, makes him as much an anti-hero as Frank Merriwell is an idol. Yet, as a substitute on an injury-decimated team, Reade deftly performs the role of his position, a reading that is demonstrated as the language of Fitzgerald's prose develops a sense that Reade's actions are a sort of re-enactment of a collection of scripted actions—they are an example of Schechner's twice-behaved behaviors, separating his performance from "every day life" sort of actions. This is most readily apparent in the climax, when, after Reade intercepts a pass (literally performing that which Fitzgerald himself could not do at the Newman School), the plot plays out to perfection: "His pursuer was breathing heavily and Reade saw what was coming. He was going to try a diving tackle" (32). Reade does not guess what is coming, does not assume what is coming; he can *see* what is coming. The verb is one of perception. Logically speaking, there is only one way by which visual perception can lead to knowledge of what will come—when what is coming has been seen before. In other words, the narrative metaphorically concludes that Reade has "rehearsed" this scene previously. His true ability is not athleticism, but knowing each step of the scene. Consequently, he easily evades the diving tackler, as if it were all a large, choreographed episode. Again, this idea of "re-playing" is not literal but metaphoric, meant to underscore the relationship athleticism bears to performance and meant to discover a different source of the social success of the football hero. He had been a good spectator on the bench himself and he fares well at stepping into another's shoes, as his status as replacement player is yet another version of his role as actor. For Reade to be successful requires not physical strength, not a privileged body, but the ability to read(e) the plays and then perform them.

The story also demonstrates a second layer of audience in that Reade's actions have a strong, persuasive effect on the other players as well. The initial skeptical voices, those which come from the coach and the team captain, disappear from the story and are replaced by the voices of players on the field, players who are duly impressed by Reade's fine play. The accolades for Reade's actions include even the voice of the opposing team's quarterback, who calls out, "Good one, Reade" (32), appropriate applause for a job well done. The irony of the situation is that Reade's status on the field relies upon such applause. If the group of players is considered a microcosmic community and the game considered analogous to a social situation, Reade's social status certainly improves throughout the course of the game. But whereas Merriwell's narratives attempt to justify his social popularity through his more advanced abilities and through his refined behavior, Fitzgerald allows

Reade's success to appear more transparent before the reader. The consistent emphasis on his play as a constructed behavior places the social power somewhere between the hands of those rooting for him and his own ability to live up to the call to be a football hero. Thus, the fact that his social status is not grounded in any sort of natural (as in physical) structure is made plain, rather than being veiled or even denied as was so often the case in stories of Frank Merriwell's heroics.

The final touchdown scene returns the focus of the prose back to the crowd, and the initial slogan of the story is replaced by "another slogan echo[ing] down the field: 'One point—two points—three points—four points—five points. Reade! Reade! Reade!'" (33). The action and language of the story thus take place completely within two slogans, just as the game itself takes place between the bounds of the crowd. The "hold" chant at the beginning of the narrative is a call that Reade's name at the end responds to. Ultimately, the descriptions of actual game action—tackles, signals, running and passing plays, and even the metaphoric "wish-fulfillment" as Kuehl calls it (30)—exist solely for the benefit of the audience. The images of the crowd frame the story with their chants and accentuate the fact that Reade's successes are due to the effect that his actions have on the crowd's reactions. His narrative existence between the probing eyes of the audience and his ability to put on a good show give him the power to be a "substitute" not just on the field but in the minds of the crowd as well; his name is transformed into a football cheer, replacing the traditional "Rah! Rah! Rah!" and making him the focus of what could be described as a mass culture rally.

An important point to emphasize is that Fitzgerald, though extremely precocious, could not have fully grasped the comprehensive nature of the complex relationship between sports and performance at the early age of fourteen. For all the emphasis on audience, crowd, and performance of a football game, Reade, the character, does not really do anything as a result of his successful victory. That is, while the community of the players and fans may be an analogy to larger social situations, Reade as a character never explicitly utilizes the status he is granted outside of the bounds of the game. Thus while the story begins to pry apart the logic behind the stock narratives of success-based social status, it nevertheless is just a quick sketch written by a budding author. Interestingly enough, as "Reade, Substitute Right Half" is beginning to demonstrate the depiction of a football game as a spectacle played before various audiences, it also exhibits a sense of romantic fantasy that most certainly came right out of the Merriwell stories. Reade is an inspirational hero of sorts, a model of success for the young boy considered too small or too ordinary to succeed.

Yet the literary genealogical lines that we can draw between the two narratives actually reinforce the way that both the football game, as well as the mass-market medium, function as a social performance. "Reade, Substitute Right Half" was written in 1910, when Patten was still churning out at least one story each week. While Reade may be a prototype for Fitzgerald himself (in much the same way that his poem "Football" was an example of "telling about it" instead of actually doing it), he can also be seen as a reincarnation of Frank Merriwell, a character who was often portrayed playing prep school football for several years before his days at Yale. In this way, Reade's story becomes a performance on another level; he plays the part of a young Merriwell, reenacting his successes. In fact, the substitution which he makes is not just a substitution for an injured player or a social substitution in the mind of the spectators, but a literary one himself. Reade is a "substitute" for Merriwell, thus allowing him to assume a role that would, theoretically, lead to not just athletic successes, but perhaps the same social accomplishments that Merriwell was given in his stories. We could even say that this story is Fitzgerald's first read(e)ing of Patten, substituting his own anti-hero for Patten's fictional idol to see what the effects might be within the probing eyes of the crowd. Fitzgerald was only 14 years old at the time, but he was already using his writing as a stage for stepping into roles, constructing a hero that would, by reductive logic, be endowed with all that Frank Merriwell had achieved at Yale; in other words, Reade's performance is both on the field and off. He paradoxically is practicing social emulation through Fitzgerald's act of storytelling. Because the emphasis is on action as performance, "Reade, Substitute Right Half" is the first step towards a more analytical and complex understanding of the composition making up the narrative of the hero figure's social prestige.

THE DRAMATIC SIDE OF THE WORK: THE YALE BOWL

In the first of his 1936 "Crack-Up" essays, Fitzgerald writes about "not being big enough (or good enough) to play football in college" and how that failure "resolved [itself] into childish waking dreams of imaginary heroism" (70). By calling his dreams of heroism "childish," Fitzgerald's introspective essay moves the force of the images away from "college" and back to his apprentice days of penning a story such as "Reade." In the essay he goes on to note that his dreams "were good enough to go to sleep on in restless nights" (70), a statement which is significant in and of itself, but has added importance when analyzed according to the specific textual location that the discussion of these old football dreams occupies within the bounds of this essay. Fitzgerald's references to his athletic failures make up the first distinctly delineated biographical episode in the essay, a passage which follows a lengthy and sometimes circumlocutious introduction. The introduction ends with a sentence which textually bridges his discussion of life with his discussion of his childish football dreams: "Of course, all life is a process of breaking down, but the blows that do the *dramatic* side of the work . . . don't show their effect all at once" (69; emphasis added). His early experiences with the game of football were dramatic, both literally and metaphorically, and they planted a seed of anxiety that developed into the incessant drive to valorize as well as simultaneously dissect the football hero. In fact, he sees his childish dreams as ones of "imaginary heroism," a phrase which carries more significance than just being a flowery way of calling his dreams unreal. Fitzgerald seems to sense that the blows in his life, specifically the inability to make the college football team, has sewn the seeds that allowed him to postulate the degree to which heroism was based upon a sense of fantasy; his idea of what constituted "heroism" was starting to take shape as nothing more than a mere label attached to football stars as a ritual and a reward, a sort of social capital. Yet perhaps precisely because they were "dramatic," these experiences gave Fitzgerald the material he utilized in his fiction as he sought to interrogate not just what "heroism" was, but how it encouraged (albeit problematically so) systems of social hierarchy. Fitzgerald's inability to make the team at Princeton thus ensured that his later attempts at the football story would be less romantic than "Reade, Substitute Right Half"; instead they would probe more deeply the issues of audience, spectator, and social consequence, and explore the sometimes paradoxical nature of the social power resulting from the social interaction between players and fans.

Fitzgerald's next major football story was the 1928 piece, "The Bowl," composed for *The Saturday Evening Post*. Fitzgerald biographies discuss the unusual trouble he had writing what was initially a "two-part, sophisticated football story" that turned into "just an awful mess" (Mellow 300). In terms of critical attention to this story—the tale of Dolly Harlan and his love-hate affair with the Princeton football team and with the game that eventually helps him win the Hollywood starlet Daisy Cary—the only detailed, analytical study is Bryant Mangum's "Distant Idols: Fate and the Work Ethic in 'The Bowl.'" Mangum's thorough exploration of the text is significant in its attention to descriptive style and to Fitzgerald's portrayal of physical action. His argument is that the story can be read, stylistically, as an attempt to "understand the symbolic and mythic components of the game" and that it serves as "a reconsideration of the romantic hero and of the heroic quest itself" (109). Just as important as the symbolic connections which Mangum identifies, however, are the social ones; the figure of the "hero," precisely because he is engaged in such a culturally significant activity as college foot-ball, is based not only in the mythic traditions which Mangum identifies but simultaneously in contemporary social practices, practices which base themselves in the ritualistic practices of the myths which Mangum identi-fies. Dolly Harlan's status as ancient mythic hero/modern football idol is the key to reading this story, a story which, at its end, is a commentary on the illusory nature of social prestige and status and the habitual inability of the hero figure to recognize the dependency his elite position has in the adula-tion of the spectators.

"The Bowl" begins, much as "Reade, Substitute Right Half" does, by immediately calling attention to the notion of an audience. Jeff Deering, the narrator who functions as both participant and observer much the same way as Nick does in *The Great Gatsby*, describes himself as one who "reveled in football, *as audience*," and before even beginning to tell the story at hand, Deering makes note of a fellow classmate who "was once unresponsive to the very *spectacle* at his door" (6; emphasis added). These words create, in a way similar to the initial scene of "Reade, Substitute Right Half," a sense of social communication between the crowd and the players. The crowd is the frame of the story, and while "performance" certainly means more than merely being watched, the fact that the narrator very purposefully notes that he is not a football player, but a fan, puts the reader in the position of seeing the "spectacle" of football "as audience" alongside the narrator. Fitzgerald's liter-ary audience is thus poised to, through the course of their reading, evaluate whether or not *they* will consider the story's hero in the same light as the fic-tional social crowds will. As Deering continues, he keeps his narrative focus on the audience, describing a fan that drunkenly yells out "'Stob Ted Coy!' under the impression that we were watching a game played a dozen years before" (6). The humor of the incident almost overshadows the representa-tion of the game as one that is rehearsed, again in a sense similar to the ways that Reade's performances appeared built upon a series of repetitive, "twice-behaved" behaviors. The action on the field, far from being a unique athletic accomplishment, appears more as a replay, as if the players themselves have scripted their movements, playing the part of Ted Coy over and over again, while the fans, too, have their typical reactions and re-enact their own parts as well. The "communication" that takes place between crowd and audience, in this way, becomes part social interaction and part ritual, a fantasy of social performance that is imagined by the narrative as a retelling of games from years past.

Deering, as narrator, also astutely perceives Dolly Harlan's feelings towards his own actions, revealing Dolly's deep-seated discontent with being a football player. Dolly's dissatisfaction with the game goes well beyond his dislike of training and the monotony of the game, partially coming out of his crippling agoraphobia within the Yale Bowl. It is significant that Yale's bowl-shaped stadium, built in 1914 with its enclosed, oval space, resembles the ancient Roman Coliseum, where "sporting events" were in actuality grand-scale spectacles with gladiators "acting and performing" for the crowd much as football players do in contemporary culture. More importantly, the archi-tecture of the stadium provides a visual image of the narrative structures of the story. The shape of the bowl stadium signifies the audience framing the characters, and, as Dolly describes to Deering at one point, when he faced an athletic situation such as fielding a punt

> the sides of that damn pan would seem to go shooting up . . . then when the ball started to come down, the sides began leaning forward and bending over me until I could see all the people on the top seats screaming at me and shaking their fists. (6)

The language of the passage moves from the physical, fixed body of the stadium to the organic body of the crowd, the latter substituting for the former. Given this imagery, then, titling the story "The Bowl" is way of leading the reader towards the audience, as if the story were titled "The Crowd" or "The Specta-tors." According to this logic, this is, very literally, the story of an audience.

Yet the stadium is only partly to blame for Dolly's discomfort in his role. As Fitzgerald writes, Dolly sometimes "imagined that a man here and there was about to tear off the mask and say, 'Dolly, do you hate this lousy business as much as I do?'" (6). The meaning of the word "mask" could be nothing more than a reference to the players' helmets, were it not for the fact that face masks were not in widespread use until the 1960s and were virtually unknown during the 1920s—helmets were usually just leather headcover-ings with a chinstrap. Thus the image of "tear[ing] off the mask" finds its meaning in connections to performance—perhaps a reference to the Greek mask of drama—and underscores the usage of athletic prowess for a rhetori-cally guided purpose; the players put on a show for their cheering audience in return for social prestige. Underlying Dolly's distress, then, is the knowl-edge, perhaps even subconscious, that he cannot tear off his mask and reveal the actor behind the role; to do so would be to risk his social position. He instead must perpetually wear it to maintain the façade, athletic and social, which the crowd expects of him.

Though these connections between the language of drama and Fitzger-ald's world of football may be intriguing, they are not significant in and of themselves. However, when placed within the larger context of the social structure portrayed in "The Bowl," the social relationships between the Bowl's audience and the hero-in-training Dolly become more complex as the players and fans interact more. After Dolly meets young socialite Vienna Thorne and sets about trying to impress her, Deering makes the following statement:

> I've put down as well as I can everything I can remember about the first meeting between Dolly and Miss Vienna Thorne. Reading it over, it sounds casual and insignificant, but the evening lay in the shadow of the game and all that happened seemed like that. (93)

The entire action of the football game, from the initial introduction of the crowd to the triumphant freshmen trying to carry Dolly off the field at the end of the day, has an aura that, through this metaphor of the shadow, reaches beyond itself and influences the way that Dolly, Deering, Vienna, and others in this social microcosm react to one another. Though he is far from extraordinary in the overall course of the game, Dolly makes a single play that turns out to be the game-winner, making him an integral part of the show. And, as the primary factor in that which casts the "shadow of the game," Dolly is entitled to some of the social prestige. It is for this reason that he initially seems confused at his inability to impress Vienna by talking about football; after all, if she had been present in the Bowl, she would have been part of the crowd granting him social prestige. But Dolly soon learns that Vienna had not seen his performance. "I see," he remarks, as if it is a foregone conclusion that despite his scorn for the football mask, he still knows how persuasive he was on the field, and how impressed Vienna would have been, had she witnessed what he had done.

What is even more important is that the "shadow" of the game is not entirely one of epic, ritualistic struggle and conquest; though Mangum rightly perceives that the mythic undertones, the ritual re-enactment of putting on the mask, bringing home the victory, and celebrating with the adoring crowds are part of the source of Dolly's power, Fitzgerald points out the limitations of the actual game experience. For the game itself, once complete, is transposed in terms of medium; that is, the game moves away from the action on the field and into the headlines of the daily paper, "nicely mounted now in the setting of the past" (93). The sport is no longer an action but instead becomes a historical record through the act of writing about it. On one hand, the emerging mass media circulation acted as a cultural object of social interaction, allowing even greater masses of people to participate in and identify with the spectacle of the game of football. More significantly, the development of the modern sports page went hand in hand with the mass spectacle that football was becoming at the time. Headlines and suc- cinct reports were features of the sporting report, and games were repre- sented through box scores and statistics. In the papers "it was not like the afternoon" at all; it was not written as a physical battle. Instead, the sports page makes the narrative of the game "succinct, condensed and clear" (93). Michael Oriard provides compelling evidence for the notion that most peo- ple, in fact, discovered football through newspaper accounts (*Reading Foot- ball* xx), accounts which recreated the narratives of the game and allowed even larger masses of people to participate as fans and engross themselves in the social conversation between spectator and player. The stories in the sports pages literally framed Dolly as a hero, editing his performance to the point where the only acts "witnessed" by the crowd of the newspaper audience are those which earn him more social capital. Because Dolly's story of athletic performance as represented by newspaper recaps exists not in terms of the action—not in terms of the process—but purely in terms of the result, the social prestige heaped upon the football idol is, while not unreal, nevertheless a "fantasy." The spectators, for all their control of the social situation, wor- ship Dolly as an idol based on the "condensed" details of the game, ignoring much of his "behavior," and it is this fact that is one of the problems Deering sees in Dolly's status as hero.

Expounding on this idea further, Deering muses upon the relationship between what people see (or read) and what they believe. As he puts it,

> I wondered if all things that screamed in the headlines were simply arbi- trary accents. As if people should ask, "What does it look like?"
>
> "It looks most like a cat."
>
> "Well, then, let's call it a cat." ("The Bowl" 93)

This language develops an important homology between Deering's internal thoughts and what he has just seen (and, again, read) concerning Dolly's football prowess. The athletic performance, as it is described second-hand in the newspaper reports, is successful in convincing the audience to bestow social prestige on Dolly—his supposed feats of strength and skill are called by what they *look* like, not by what they are. In fact, that Fitzgerald would create his hero to be, really, a fair-to-middling athlete who benefits from a single flash of greatness is in some ways his way of undermining the idea that natural, physical talent is all one needs to succeed, whether in football or in a community. Keep in mind that the significance of this passage is not in claiming that Dolly is being deceitful—first of all, the very nature of athletic competition demands that at least in some sense, the outcome is determined a bit by chance. Instead of setting up football performance as a fraud, then, the story is setting it up as a *social construction*—the combination of a little fortune, a good story line (the kind a newspaper account would have), and an environment purposefully created for the act of playing football.

Dolly makes an attempt to remove himself from the social system of the spectacle of football, primarily at the behest of Vienna whose spell he has fallen under. His methodology for getting off the team is to break his own ankle, presumably to avoid having to put on the mask for another show. It is important to note that he attacks the physical part of his ability to perform on the gridiron, almost as if he knows that the "weakest" factor involved in being a good football player is physical ability, despite the fact that physical superiority is what the crowds value. But once he is unable to play football, Dolly realizes what he has truly lost. For Dolly, without football there is no status. "[I]t was Vienna's party," remarks Deering, implying that Dolly has become nothing more than an accessory for Vienna to cart around and introduce to *her* friends, friends who think Dolly dull and never ask him about his "specialty" (94). No longer ascending the social ladder, Dolly, despite such disdain for football in previous school years, begins to be "awfully curious" about the weekly fate of the Princeton team. Deering calls Dolly one "who had always been going somewhere with dynamic indolence," one who "once created groups—groups of classmates who wanted to walk with him, of underclassmen who followed with their eyes a moving shrine" (94). The image of a large body of nameless students following one football star is hauntingly reminiscent of Amory's vision of Allenby and his marching phalanx, an archetype of Princeton's social system. This is what Dolly is missing by substituting Vienna for football stardom; this is what he gets by taking off "the mask." He has moved from the position of hero or idol to the position of spectator, and he seems unable to adjust to his new role in the social interaction.

In looking for literary ancestors, Dolly as a character, then, akin to *This Side of Paradise*'s Allenby, is *not* a descendant of Frank Merriwell. Or perhaps more accurately, Dolly Harlan's lack of status among Vienna's friends demonstrates the ironies involved in creating a social hierarchy around a narrative of supposed merit-based success. If Dolly's renown early in the story had been based on some sort of measurable ability, it would not be so fleeting. Moreover, the change in Dolly's social position—in terms of moving to the center of social attention rather than in terms of rising in class "position"—discounts Merriwell's statements about equality in opportunity at football. The characteristics emphasized in Dolly Harlan are those of being an idol and having a loyal following rather than being only one of many who have the opportunity to succeed. Remember that Frank was oblivious to the fact that his perpetual role at the top of the social ladder belies his own testimony of an ideal of the "poorest" boy being able to become an "idol." Merriwell was in a protected position; he knew that the spectators valued his athletic ability, so for him to claim that others could achieve the same would only serve to bolster his status rather than foster social equality. Dolly, as another of Fitzgerald's un-Merriwellian heroes, loses his protected position when he stops playing the game, almost as if Dolly is a challenge to the justification that those of elite status try to create for their prestige.

Despite the critiques of the status groups formed through football success and stardom, Fitzgerald nevertheless *still* feels, in some ways, the allure of being the hero. To this end, the story isn't satisfied with dissecting the various aspects of Dolly's social performances. Deering comments, "people want their idols a little above them" (94), and yet with Vienna, Dolly "had been a sort of private and special idol" (94). The form of idol which Vienna makes of Dolly, as "private," is the antithesis of the sort of hero that the hyper-public space of the football stadium created out of Dolly. Ultimately, Dolly feels the pull of the public adoration and cannot resist the pull of the great gridiron stage. The newspaper accounts, that same medium which had convinced the masses that Dolly was deserving of their worship, fuel Dolly's drive to return to the system of social hierarchy (at least the system where he is at the top as opposed to the one where Vienna is). He surrounds himself with "all the sporting pages of all the papers" (97), creating a sort of "bowl" stadium in his room. Off the team and unable to execute the physical actions that a football player normally does, Dolly substitutes other forms of physical movement through his spectatorship. He gradually gets closer and closer to the game, represented through the descriptions of Dolly physically moving down the stadium at each game.

Finally, Dolly makes the decision to return to the team. Vienna, repulsed by such a decision, tries to expose the fact that Dolly is just playing a part in hopes of receiving social prestige. She bitterly says to him,

> You're weak and you want to be admired. This year you haven't had a lot of little boys following you around as if you were Jack Dempsey, and it almost breaks your heart. You want to get out in front of them all and make a show of yourself and hear the applause. (97)

Vienna's language, when placed in juxtaposition with Dolly's decision to pick social status of the mass audience over Vienna, exhibit a contradiction that perhaps lies in Fitzgerald himself. Obviously, the purpose of this paragraph is to "expose," in that it very explicitly labels the football player a "performer," one who "make[s] a show" of himself. Yet while Fitzgerald in some ways might identify with Vienna's position, especially due to his earlier characterization of Dolly, he also identifies with Dolly's desires for that status, regardless of whether or not it is built on the fantasy of a constructed performance. Principles aside, power is power. As Vienna very astutely notes, "he prefers football to [her]" (97). This tension between abstract notions of communal status and more individualized relationships do not contradict the criticism of Patten's ideas of what constitutes social success, and in fact demonstrates that Fitzgerald never calls football-based social success unreal.

But he still doesn't see Dolly as a "hero" in the sense that Patten wanted Merriwell to be. To solidify this argument, the text introduces the figure of Hollywood starlet Daisy Cary to serve as a sort of metonymy for acquired social power. Choosing to leave Vienna and be with Daisy, Dolly returns to the Princeton team as a player. In essence, he is on some level going to do just what Daisy asked him: "if he'd like to be in a *football picture* she was going to make" (97, emphasis added). What better picture could there be to achieve the results which Dolly was not only seeking, but which the sports pages had convinced him that he deserved? In consistent fashion, Deering the narrator eloquently captures the scene with language reminiscent of the way in which the story began:

> The actual day of the game was, as usual, like a dream—unreal with its crowds of friends and relatives and the inessential trappings of a gigantic show. The eleven little men who ran out on the field at last were like bewitched figures in another world, strange and infinitely romantic, blurred by a throbbing mist of people and sound. (100)

The scene is one of fantasy, one in which the men among whom Dolly chooses to be, characterized as "infinitely romantic" (the same phrase used to describe Allenby in *This Side of Paradise*) are "unreal" idols for the crowd lost in their dream-like reverie. Again, in this sense unreal does *not* mean illusory, but it means un-natural—it is not everyday experience, or a common social interaction. Instead the encounter between the fans in The Bowl and the players on the field is described as a ritual, with the athletes being "bewitched figures in another world," god-like figures surrounded by a sort of mystic worship represented by the image of the "throbbing mist."

Significantly, the fact that it is a "gigantic show" does not undermine the tangible results of this fantasy. Four quarters later, Dolly has completed the performance of a lifetime, aided, once again through pure fortune that this time takes the form of an errant pass. Dolly first and foremost knows he'll "be in the headlines tomorrow" (100). Though Fitzgerald consistently characterized Dolly Harlan as everything which Frank Merriwell was not, the end result is the same—both win the game with some last second "heroics." Dolly, one "who had scarcely carried the ball a dozen times in his Princeton career," does not need great athletic ability. He is still returned to the position of idol, in terms of the football game and in terms of the social relationships. Dolly's status in the end is based in fantasy rather than, as Patten would assert, his physical skill, since the mass audience desires winning even above talent and performance.

And what is more, Dolly's ability to put on a show of athletic prowess translates into the social prowess that he felt missing in his relationship with Vienna. It cements his position with Daisy Cary, another star-like figure who, according to Mangum, "accepts Dolly as an idol as she accepts her own role. Theirs was a community of idols separate from the community of idolaters" (116). The concluding scene is the signature moment of the story; passing through the crowd of people clamoring to meet the young Hollywood beauty, Dolly is asked why he is being so presumptuous as his attempts to see Daisy in her hotel room. After all, reasons the crowd who has accorded Dolly so much acclaim, no one else has been accorded the privilege. "Just who are you?" a voice cries ("The Bowl" 100). Dolly's reaction summarizes what he has accomplished through his masterful performance and, more importantly, what Fitzgerald recognizes about the ultimate role that a football game has as a form of social communication and interaction: "He felt as if life had arranged his role to make possible this particular question—a question that now he had no choice but to answer" (100). Dolly's mind set is such that he believes he only needs to call out his name. And, just as Reade's name, called out at the conclusion of the earlier story, became a chant and a cheer, the refrain "Why, I'm Dolly Harlan" is the culmination of the performance that allows Dolly to assume the "image of victory and pride" that reclaims for him the position at the top of the elite ladder (100). "The Bowl" is not a hero story in the way that "Reade, Substitute Right Half" is, but it is a hero story in the sense that Dolly Harlan finds his social success through athletic activity. It is almost as if "The Bowl" is a story of a figure characterized in every way as an anti-hero who, ultimately, becomes what others have made him into, accepting and assuming the role of idol.

TO BE FINE ACTORS IN ANY CASE

"The Bowl" was written between *The Great Gatsby* and *Tender is the Night*, eighteen years after "Reade, Substitute Right Half" when Fitzgerald was no longer an aspiring, "apprentice" author but was at the proverbial height of his stylistic career. As such, it demonstrates more complex thinking about the nature of the power structures surrounding the playing of football. It is also a much more mature and a better story stylistically, a fact which again can be attributed to experience. In sharp contrast, the final football story of Fitzgerald's career, "'Send Me In, Coach,'" does not in any way evidence the same type of growth in formalistic style, even though it was published eight years after "The Bowl." Written for *Esquire* magazine for only $250, it would be difficult for anyone to claim this piece as a masterful Fitzgerald story. Even Fitzgerald showed no liking for the story himself, in fact marking it "scrap" in November of 1936 (Higgins 165). But despite its stylistic shortcomings and banal, worn-out dialogue, when read in conjunction with the two previous stories it demonstrates the philosophical progression in Fitzgerald's attempts to uncover the convoluted relationship between football and performance. Through the course of the story, even though Fitzgerald still exhibits a sort of nostalgic longing for the youthful acceptance of the football idol, he also much more fully realizes, even more so than in "The Bowl," his critiques of the ways in which the idol garners his status. The story serves in some way as a capstone to his literary responses to the influence of Frank Merriwell on the genre of the football story; as Fitzgerald continues to scrutinize the connections between football, performance, and status, this final narrative articulates the notion that just as there is no true equality in opportunities for athletic success, there is no true equality in opportunities for social success.

The exposition of the story is much more direct in calling attention to the language and setting of performance than the previous stories. Most significantly, the scene is set at a boys' camp where the young men, rather than playing sports, are rehearsing a play about football. The literary genre of the story is not narrative prose, but instead is formalistically a drama, complete with stage directions and a cast of characters. Football is thus immediately positioned as a rehearsed set of behaviors, a staged construction based on the culmination of practices and on the intersection with the crowd. The characters and plot are fairly basic and easily understood. The first two boys introduced, Bugs and Cassius, are respectively "small, undersized" and "stout, overgrown" (34)—two extremes of what Fitzgerald might label (at that age) the social outcast. The boys, who are later joined by two others, Henry and Bill, worship their head counselor Rickey. The story characterizes Rickey as a promising football star, working at the summer camp to make some money while deciding where to go to college in the fall. The final character is the "Old Man," who is the director of the boys' camp as well as the director of the play. Significantly, the Old Man is set to be the coach of the state college in the fall; the initial conflict is thus set up as the Old Man attempts to convince Rickey that it is in his best interests to come play for him in the fall.

The central figure of both Fitzgerald's story and the fictional play which the boys are rehearsing is Bill, who is taking on the role of Playfair, the star player. Bill is even more the antithesis of Frank Merriwell than Reade or Dolly Harlan. He is a young boy filled with inadequacies and inabilities, social missteps which he exhibits throughout the story. Bill's age, combined with the time setting of the story, puts him in the class of the young boys who might have been in Gilbert Patten's implied audience. As such, Bill is a boy searching for idols. Significantly, though, even if Merriwell's world of meritocracy were valid, Bill is in no way blessed with the talent that would allow him to succeed in such a social system. Hence the setting of the football play; instead of spending the summer at a traditional summer camp, one based in physical activity (including a heavy emphasis on team sports which traditional camps usually exhibit), Bill is at an acting camp. Fitzgerald has written, in the character of Bill, an outsider who is striving to find a way to move to the center of social acceptance; Bill's is yet another story of the search for social mobility.

Bill has a desire for social accolades; he has a sense of upward movement and of trying to get ahead in life. He chides the other boys at his rehearsal for goofing off, saying, "since our parents have spent money to send us here I think we should take advantage of every single advantage that we have while we are here" (41). Yet in talking about a word having such socially charged significance as "advantage," Bill is quick to point out that it is not money that grants the advantages, but performance. He continues, "now this is a play that's supposed to teach us how to be fine actors in the future or if we don't want to be fine actors—well to be fine actors in any case" (41). Bill sees at this early stage the importance of being a fine actor even if you are not literally planning on going onto the stage; performance is a rhetoric that reaches far beyond the genre of drama. Given the setting of the story itself, readers might be led to the conclusion that the simple football play which Bill so fondly rehearses will eventually lead him to the success he wants in life. Because he understands the nature of performance as an "advantage," it would be tempting to imagine him as a younger version of Dolly Harlan, acquiring the skills of wearing "the mask" in such a way as to solidify his prominence and right to privilege by winning over the crowds that might gather to watch him. It is also tempting to see him, in some ways, akin to Amory Blaine, taking pains to observe others and strive to emulate their behavior, modeling himself after the heroes in order to be a hero. Such arguments make Bill a complex combination of both spectatorship and emulation, watching in order to be able to later perform.

But as we learn more about Bill and his own interaction with his idol, these simplified comparisons between Bill and previous Fitzgerald anti-heroes become more complicated. Bill, like so many of Fitzgerald's young boys, does yearn to be able to have the type of social prowess that his idol—in this case counselor Rickey—does: "I think Mr. Rickey is the most wonderful man in the world. . . . If I could ever be like Mr. Rickey just once" (43). But the real crux of young Bill's dreams, and that which makes this story more than just a poor re-invention of what Fitzgerald has already written, is that he does not want to be the type of *athlete* that Rickey is. The heart of the cultural text of football which Fitzgerald has been interrogating is the degree to which a character can use athletics to enter into the system of social privilege which, from the outside, is so tempting. But Bill knows that he "can never be as great" an athlete as counselor Rickey. Instead, he wants to be like him "just once" (43). In other words, he just wants to spend a bit of time in Rickey's shoes—he wants to play the part of Rickey. He wants to, metaphorically speaking, just be a substitute. Bill's goal of emulation thus differs from Reade's or Dolly's, in that his aspirations are not for the social status that comes through successful athletic performance. By setting a goal to merely perform as an idol, young Bill effectively argues against the Merriwellian formula for success. In some ways, Bill is thus a demonstration of the ways which the mass culture phenomenon of the player-fan interaction completely collapses the distinction between being an idol and appearing to be an idol, putting the ritual of idol-worship on tenuous ground. Not tenuous in terms of unreal or lacking power, but in terms of the ability of idol worship to actually foster the "democratic spirit" of football which Merriwell so consistently argued for. For Bill to want, literally, to play the part of a football star in order to be the idol "just once" is a recognition that the status of the hero is itself nothing more than a fiction based on performance.

In fact, Fitzgerald, through his characterization of Bill, expands on some of his critiques of the idol figure, refining his ideas concerning the ways in which an idol's status is based in substitution. Just as the fans who gather together at a football stadium unite in their cheering, their support, and their worship as a sort of worship and also vicarious participation, allowing those demonstrating the physical strength and skill to stand for that which they desire to do themselves, Bill wants Rickey to succeed as a football star rather than doing so himself, so that Rickey's success would then extend to him as he tries to be like him just once. From the spectator's point of view, this makes the act of emulation an act of mental substitution, and from the hero's point of view, football performance is more a matter of "telling about it," to use Fitzgerald's phrase from "Author's House" about the substitutive powers of literature. It's about making oneself "as big a hit" as if you were able to perform some other sort of social behavior.

Bill invests himself in the small camp production as a way of believing that he can be like Rickey. In fact, he tells the Old Man that he wants his life to be "like in the play" (43). Bill feels that through his rehearsals he is also able to assume the athletic talent and social consequences of Playfair, the stage equivalent of Rickey, a star whom each character in the play adores and who, during the course of a given game, "would take the pigskin and before anyone had known it would run the full length of the field" (39). Playfair's name is just as significant to the story's relationship to the conventional football narrative as is Reade's. Bill's task as the story opens is to attempt to step into the shoes of the archetypal football star who extols the virtues of "playing fair"; in other words, he is performing as a substitute for Frank Merriwell.

In setting Bill up in such a manner, Fitzgerald constructs the boy as the type of figure who, in his youth, seems fully to understand how to be socially persuasive through athletics. Fitzgerald also sets up an interesting juxtaposition with the object of Bill's adulation. Rickey, though a great athlete himself who "could throw a pass like a baseball forty-five yards" (38), is already twenty years old and despite his athletic abilities and despite what young Bill thinks of him, feels that his own skills on the gridiron lack the type of heroic significance to make the crowds respond to him in the way that an idol ought to.

More importantly, Rickey, too, utterly lacks any sense of the social prestige that the other fictional football stars we've been examining in this chapter are able to acquire. Rickey learned to play football on his own, without any coaching; but, through the course of the narrative Rickey reveals that by playing on his own, away from a community of players—away from the "eleven other boys that learned the game in normal school" (38)—he wasn't able to develop much in the way of social skills. Rickey is Fitzgerald's first example of a football player who has strength, speed, and tangible athletic ability, ability which is as naturally inherent as any. Yet Rickey is just as much of a social outcast as Bill is, thus forcefully undermining the Merriwell formula. Fitzgerald uses images of the violent nature of football to demonstrate the ways in natural, physical talent in Rickey's case doesn't add up to the same sort of social status which the worshipping crowds heap upon the stars from the other stories this chapter looks at. In trying to resist the Old Man's pleadings for Rickey to play for him, Rickey mentions that the other players on the state team—those who are out there wearing Dolly's mask—never show any overt signs of having been in any sort of mythic battle. They are the fiction of football, testifying that the game is a big show and that the action and the storylines take precedence over the physicality and brutality of actual football games.

Because of what they have done through their play, these other boys appear in the social world in much the same way that an account of a football game appears in the newspapers—they "come out clean" (38). They show no traces of having been in the game; injuries are not real, bodies are left intact—while Rickey sits at home with "marks all over [his] face" (37). For all the subtle differences between Frank Merriwell and Fitzgerald's heroes, Reade and Dolly, the one place in which they would all agree is in the idea that the images of the successful football idol, constructed upon a set of performance behaviors that draw the crowd into a venerative relationship, stays separate from the violent underpinnings of the game.

Yet the cultural significance of this particular story, that which makes it, in some way, the culmination of Fitzgerald's football stories, is that Rickey represents the vision of the football idol outside of the social structure, and thus in some ways outside of the performance. Rickey would sit at home with his "nose broken Sunday, Monday and Tuesday" (37–8). But the other players, those who look good at what they do, garner social accolades from their ability to avoid the marks of their performance. They "get two thousand, five thousand, ten thousand" dollars, instead of the mere board and tuition Rickey is offered (37). These players are those who are able to "take the sorority girls out in the night-time" (38). This tension which Fitzgerald sets up between Rickey, the one with real talent but unable to capitalize on his performance, and the other football stars, clearly successful socially as well as athletically, might even be read as a sort of glimpse of Fitzgerald's assessment of his own washed-up status. The signs of success which Rickey mentions to the Old Man, money and women, were always, for Fitzgerald, the ultimate signification of having made it socially. Again coming back to this idea of the story as a refinement of the idea of "telling about it" substitution, Fitzgerald is using Rickey's physical talent as a metaphor for his own writing abilities and Rickey's inability to be the type of football "performer" as a way of arguing that he, Fitzgerald, is no longer able to "play the game" of being the idol—the celebrity—which he tried to be for so much of his writing career. Thus football performance, a concept which Fitzgerald considered throughout his life, is, in this story, finally not even as much about the details of the sport as it is about his own inability to reconcile the concept of social acceptance and demonstrable talent.

Both Fitzgerald's story and the fictional play-with-the-text have their inconsistencies that, in some sense, make some critics place "'Send Me In, Coach,'" quite low on their scale of "quality literature." Matthew Bruccoli, for example, opted to exclude the story from *The Price Was High,* an anthology which was designed to collect all of Fitzgerald's remaining uncollected short stories. Quite a bit about the story is, you might say, over the top in "dramatic" ways. These details include such observations that at times Playfair is a football star, at others he's a baseball star. Yet on one level this is a confusion that actually lends itself to supporting the idea of athletic "performance"; touchdown passes or triple plays may make a difference in the sporting world, but not in the social world, and Playfair is loved for them all. Other moments of disorder may seem much more exasperating, yet the moments of confusion make the story as much a glimpse of Fitzgerald's own social situation as does his characterization of Rickey. Cassius constantly forgets his lines and Bugs cannot keep his mind on the play/game, preferring instead to write the word "wedoodle" again and again on the blackboard. The premise behind the rehearsal is abruptly interrupted when Fitzgerald has Bill learning that his father has just shot himself—news that seems as out of place to the readers as it does to Bill, who just wants to go on with his acting. While such details might tempt us to read the story as an irritating, quickly written mess, and while the story may appear tedious stylistically, when taken in conjunction with the other two football stories it is clear was Fitzgerald was at least attempting to do. The story is incredibly revealing in its confusions; Fitzgerald performs as himself in this story, attempting to tell about the struggles, obstacles, and distractions he faced in trying to be the "football" idol, even just once.

Part Rickey, part Playfair, and part Bill, Fitzgerald used the juxtaposition of these characters to represent a conclusion that he kept pursuing throughout his career, an answer to the unstated questions he might have had about the football hero fiction of Gilbert Patten or others. In the character of Bill, we see an understanding of how to be an athlete that Frank

Merriwell never quite comprehends. In contrast to all of Merriwell's abilities to win over the observing spectators through his performance as a football player, Bill never wins the game on the final play. Nevertheless he calls himself "useful," perhaps a more fitting appellation than the word which had such significance for Merriwell as well as for Dolly Harlan, "idol."

Chapter Four

"Perfunctory Patriotism": Tom Buchanan, Meyer Wolfshiem, and "America's Game"

While conversing privately with Nick in chapter four of *The Great Gatsby*, Jay Gatsby makes an offer to clear up some of the stories which, as Nick has already discovered, were being spread concerning Gatsby's rise to fortune. "I don't want you to get a wrong idea of me from all these stories you hear," he tells Nick. Gatsby then, in an effort to provide tangible evidence of his history, proceeds to empty his pockets with "souvenirs" that he conveniently has on hand. One of these objects is "a photograph of half a dozen young men in blazers loafing in an archway through which were visible a host of spires" (53). As Nick studies the photograph, he discerns that standing among the gentlemen is "Gatsby, looking a little, not much, younger—with a cricket bat in his hand" (53). This photograph, following on the heels of Gatsby's stories and shining medals, opens Nick's eyes and is that which convinces him, at least according to our knowledge as reader, that he believes that Gatsby's story of himself "was all true."

As was the case with *This Side of Paradise* and with some of his short stories, Fitzgerald here uses an association with sport as a crucial piece in fashioning his "social fiction," to use Brian Way's term. *The Great Gatsby* is a novel that is (among other things) a 1920s experiment in depicting the contentions and ambivalences between the upper class and the middle class over what best represents America. Lionel Trilling once called it a book that, like the character of Gatsby, is most "peculiarly American" (15); more precisely, it is an attempt to explore tensions between different groups of people all calling themselves American. To this end, the small passage concerning the Oxford photograph which Gatsby "always carr[ies]" around with him is charged with the larger conflicts of the novel, conflicts between the Buchanans' elitism and Gatsby's opulent attempt to rise from the middle class.

This is not to imply, of course, an oversimplification of class strata in the 1920s by ignoring the fact that a majority of American citizens were not of either of these two classes. The decade also exhibited enormous anxiety amongst what Michael E. Parrish calls "the other Americas": blue-collar factory workers, farm workers, recent immigrants, etc. (71–95). *The Great Gatsby*, however, favors a portrayal of leisure (or a pursuit of leisure) over work. As Bill Brown notes, "By the century's turn . . . play, not, work, appeared to be the mode through which a culture expresse[d] itself" (9). In this way, sports is partly connected to the larger evolution in terms of leisure time and leisure space as practiced in America from the turn of the century and beyond. Entertainment had evolved throughout the 19th century into a profit-turning commodity, and by the 1920s leisure was not just an activity but an industry, one central to American life. Given this observation, the novel is particularly interested in the clashes between the post-war American with the economic means to enter the world of consumerism and the pecuniary citizen who felt threatened by the burgeoning economic power of an expanding middle class. The text produces an awareness of the disconnection Fitzgerald keenly identified between two competing Americas—the glamorous upper-crust society of leisure to which he continually aspired in his personal life, and the ever-growing middle-class society that characterized his upbringing. And it is in this discord, in this photograph, where *The Great Gatsby* and sports intersect.

THE DIAMETER OF FRANK CHANCE'S DIAMOND

Implicit in chapters two and three of my argument is an observation that, when it came to sports, F. Scott Fitzgerald's strongest personal connection was to college football. His attempts to understand better the relationship which that sport bears to issues of class and community not only helped him comprehend such issues in his fiction and his life, but also repositioned football as a cultural phenomenon that is much more complex than often considered. Fitzgerald's use of football in his short stories and in *This Side of Paradise* demonstrates that spectator sports in the first part of the twentieth century challenged the commonly held misconception that sport places people on an equal footing. The complex relationship between football, social status, and community/nation building establishes that sport is often used to actively create and reinforce cultural lines of status rather than merely reflecting already existing boundaries.

However, it is intriguing that in *The Great Gatsby*, Fitzgerald's most significant novel, football plays, at best, a minor role. The single reference to that sport is the mention of Tom Buchanan as a former Yale football star. The reference is not insignificant, in that it draws on the violence inherent in game play to deepen the portrayal of Tom as a "hulking brute of a man" (13). Messenger, in discussing Tom Buchanan's status as a former Yale star, claims that Tom is "thrashing in the chains of his own boredom and restlessness, a Yale All-American end ostensibly bred for power and responsibility but reduced to the life of a country squire on Long Island" (190). Tom's description also posits a logical post-football life for the figure of Allenby from *This Side of Paradise;* Tom is what Allenby might become once removed from the romanticized, self-contained walls of the Ivy League. Nick assesses Tom as someone who "would drift on forever seeking a little wistfully for the dramatic turbulence of some irrecoverable football game" (9). These characterizations certainly use Fitzgerald's previous investigations into football as a way to set up the exposition of the novel. Yet beyond this moment, football is conspicuously absent. Conspicuous because if, as demonstrated in previous chapters, football is bound up in class, status, and nationalism, then it would seem natural for it to play a prominent role in this novel. Yet football is not the sport of *The Great Gatsby.*[1]

Instead, baseball is. Baseball figures in Fitzgerald's examination of emerging American self-characterization in a unique way. Fitzgerald is often charged with having a strong disdain for the game of baseball; in his most direct statement about his personal feelings towards the sport, Fitzgerald called baseball a "boy's game, with no more possibilities in it than a boy could master" ("Ring" 36). Fitzgerald's friendship with and critical analysis of his Long Island neighbor Ring Lardner was, in large part, responsible for critics assuming that Fitzgerald held baseball in low regard. Admittedly, Fitzgerald felt that Lardner's time spent as a traveling correspondent with the Chicago Cubs and White Sox baseball clubs had limited Lardner's growth as a writer: "However deeply Ring might cut into it, his cake had exactly the diameter of Frank Chance's diamond" (36). On some levels, Fitzgerald saw baseball as rudimentary in nature, especially when compared to college football. His words about Ring Lardner's shortcomings as a writer focus on what Fitzgerald saw as Lardner's over-reliance on baseball. Such an attitude perhaps points to Fitzgerald's own personal fear that to write about baseball himself would prevent him from achieving the complexity of social and cultural observation he sought in his literature. He calls baseball "a game bounded by walls which kept out novelty or danger, change or adventure" (36), evoking an image of a baseball stadium as a hedge of safeguarding naiveté, separating its occupants from the real world of experience.

Yet despite making such comments about baseball following Ring Lardner's death, Fitzgerald had already written about baseball in his most significant work of cultural commentary. Though *The Great Gatsby* contains only a few scattered allusions to baseball amidst its complex collection of cultural objects, these allusions are far from cursory—they are, in fact, pivotal to understanding the novel and even more pivotal to understanding the role baseball played in early twentieth century ideologies of class and nationalism. John F. Callahan, writing that "the truth about America has got to precede allegiance to any structure that has misrepresented history," calls Fitzgerald a novelist dedicated to describing the "complexity of the American" (vii). If such an assumption is true, then the appearance of the game of baseball in the novel is part of the "truth about America." Baseball functions in the novel in ways that football does not, in ways football cannot. John Lauricella argues that "the inclusion of baseball in so self-conscious an artifact of high literary art suggests that Fitzgerald's instincts as a working novelist are keener than his principles as a critic" (86), indicating that Fitzgerald's written disdain for baseball in his elegy to Ring Lardner was just an issue of personal taste, and was in no way detrimental to his ability to assess cultural importance.

By interrogating moments in the text where allusions or references to baseball intersect with the cultural history and significance of the sport, I will demonstrate how Fitzgerald used baseball—specifically, how the sport itself sheds light on his struggle to comprehend how middle-class values and aspirations clashed with those held by the higher strata to which he aspired. More importantly, by looking at what baseball reveals about the novel I will demonstrate what Fitzgerald reveals about baseball. *The Great Gatsby* shows that Fitzgerald, for all his dislike of the sport, recognized the complexities of its connection to class tension and anxiety. Ultimately, Fitzgerald understood and critiqued the way that stories told about baseball, both individual narratives as well as cultural and historical ones, evolved into tools of American nationalism, specifically a middle-class nationalism with its own ideologies of nostalgia for the supposed values which gave rise to the American nation.[2]

THE POPULARIZATION OF BASEBALL

Gatsby's photograph of his Oxford cricket-playing days is as much a product of an American cultural history as it is a British one. While it may seem remarkable in hindsight, in the 1840s and early 1850s the most popular team sport in the United States was not baseball, but was instead cricket, a game most often played by British immigrants and used as a method for the English community "to preserve its own ethnic identity" (Kirsch 97). Its popularity in the late 1840s and early 1850s stemmed primarily from the fact that the game's players were, for the most part, upper-class, wealthy businessmen who could afford leisure time in which to play and who had a taste for things associated with Britain. Kirsch notes that as economic means grew in the mid-century among a few, the mass of free time and money led some of the elite to invest their resources in sport, and those who weren't patronizing the sports of horse racing or yachting turned to cricket to satisfy their desire for sporting entertainment (6). The wealthy class could also afford more space; John C. Stevens, for example, donated the Elysian Fields in Hoboken for the development of cricket grounds.

Adding to its popularity was the fact that, by virtue of its long history, cricket was highly codified and organized. Bat and ball games had been played informally by youth in America for quite some time. Various forms of townball, games with names such as rounders, round ball, one old cat, and goal ball, were common throughout the colonial and revolutionary period (Koppett 137). However, during the rise of team sport playing in the 1840s and 1850s, when ballplaying became more common among adults, the game of cricket had resources that appealed to a mentality of making sporting endeavor more than just a diversion. Businessmen and wealthy fraternal organizations, attracted by the organization as well as inherent sociability in cricket, began forming city cricket clubs (Kirsch 21–23). The highlight of the American cricket scene was when an all-England team agreed to travel to the United States in 1859 to play American teams from Rochester, Manhattan, and Philadelphia. If antebellum participation in cricket among the wealthy classes were an accurate forecast of national sporting trends, cricket might have very soon earned the label of the national pastime.

However, in the late 1850s and into the 1860s, the popularity of cricket began to wane due in large part to cultural forces that ultimately lay outside of sport, most notably the complex intersection between social hierarchy and a growing sense of nationalism. John Higham's *Strangers in the Land,* for example, details the way that American cultural nationalism in the mid-nineteenth century was partially fostered by images of "Brother Jonathan" challenging "John Bull" in various athletic competitions, including horse racing, yachting, and boxing. Placing ideals of American superiority over other nations within the framework of sports, especially sports so traditionally considered as elite British imports, was a way to make America, as a nation, seem stronger, swifter, and more naturally gifted. When it came to cricket, the demographic and economic composition of those involved as cricket players created a particularly large obstacle for the game's spread outside of major metropolitan areas such as Philadelphia or Boston. The ethnic component of cricket playing was hostile to the developing sentiment of political and cultural nationalism in nineteenth-century America. Moreover, a sort of prejudice began to emerge against cricket playing on the grounds that it wasn't harmonious with the physical, rugged "American" spirit.

The factor which, perhaps, had the most adverse effect on cricket's popularity in America was the rapid diversification of the populations in the cities where the team sports were being played. Ironically, this same factor had a positive effect on the growth of team sports overall, because diversification led to a sort of fragmentation in terms of communities. Social relations were strained as large masses of people struggled to figure out how they fit together when there were so many differences in one's status within the society, especially in terms of economic position and/or racial and ethnic makeup. In many individuals' desires to regain a sense of group identification within the cities, communities were formed not just along lines of identity (i.e. not just neighborhoods based on wealth or ethnic background) but along lines of behavior—communities of common religious practice, of similar vocation, and so forth all blossomed. Sport was such a behavior, and thus the desire for social community had a direct influence on the rise of adult participation in team sports (Kirsch 9). Yet with the formation of sporting communities came sporting exclusion. In essence, while cricket was the most popular team sport based on participation as well as based on media coverage and money earned through a development of professionalization (two factors that were growing in importance) (98)—the fact that cricket had such an overt British heritage, and even more so was monopolized by those of British decent, fueled the fire of anti-cricket sentiment as the years rolled on.

This is a complex point to flesh out in exploring the tension between the upper-class citizens playing cricket and those who were either engaged in other forms of ball-playing or who weren't engaged in sports much at all. It would be too simplistic to say that cricket lost favor in the United States *merely* because it was a British game and Americans were trying to do things that were very visibly not British. For while that is true, the reverse is also true, in that those playing cricket were in some way trying to separate themselves from the "Americans" who wouldn't (or couldn't) play the game. Henry Chadwick, often called the father of modern sports statistics, said that cricket would fail in America not because of American prejudice, but because of "international prejudice, the majority of cricketers refusing to sacrifice their national desire for supremacy in order that the game might be made popular in America" (*Ball Players Chronicle*). William T. Porter's *The Spirit of the Times*, one of the first American periodicals devoted to sport, was more overt in criticizing cricket players for their elitist attitude, calling the game "imported snobbishness" (343). And, as mentioned earlier, even in cases where American-born citizens joined cricket clubs, such players were upper-class residents themselves and only fed into the conception of cricket as a privileged, Anglo-centric sport.

Some of the obstacles that stood in the way of cricket becoming more popular nationwide were simultaneously factors allowing baseball to emerge as a more suitable team sport for America. Specifically, while cricket was disparaged for being an aristocratic, British sport, baseball claimed the space on the other end of the spectrum, adopting the characterization of being an American sport that eschewed attitudes of elitism usually associated with England. Baseball was a sport which, at least in terms of how it was perceived, created *inclusive* community through sport, an attractive feature to those who felt that cricket was too "exclusionary" for the average American. Baseball, as codified by Alexander Cartwright and his Knicker-bocker Baseball Club, was rapidly adopted in diverse locales throughout the country as it encouraged ordinary people with ordinary jobs to band together as players with a singular competitive goal. Stephen Gelber argues that baseball "subsumed the individual into the collective" as it evolved alongside the modern industrial and business revolutions, and Warren Goldstein agrees, adding that baseball "had never been very far removed" from the world of middle-class community (qtd. in Tygiel 10). To be fair, "middle class" in the 1850s is not necessarily the same thing as "middle class" in the 1920s. My use of the term here is designed more to mean a "middle-class status," designating those who perhaps had more economic power and ability than the typical working American but who were quite markedly excluded from the world of upper-crust society. Adelman notes that the majority of baseball players before the Civil War were bankers, doctors, lawyers, clerks, and other "white-collar" citizens (122–23), workers who certainly weren't poor but who didn't enjoy the type of aristocratic, pecuniary lifestyle of the upper class. Baseball helped middle-class citizens form middle-class communities, as they played for leisure, for health, and, most importantly, for sociability.[3]

Additionally, as cricket was being perceived as a foreign, British game, baseball was casting itself as a uniquely American sport. Baseball was, in comparison to cricket, relatively simple in terms of rules; the visual symmetry of the game appealed to the modern, progressive sensibilities embraced by many of its middle-class originators; and the out and inning structure fit the compressed time available for ballplaying on the part of the middle-class workforce (cricket games were usually stretched over two days, a luxury not available to the middle-class merchants and office workers who had regular workday schedules). More importantly, as the years continued on and baseball surpassed cricket in terms of its playing population, it also proved itself to fit much better than cricket with the spectator culture that was evolving towards the latter parts of the century. The governing body of baseball as it became a "spectator sport" was the National League; the owners in the National League who profited from the professionalization of the sport saw how baseball was suited to concepts of audience and crowd and marketed it accordingly. The baseball field, with its clearly defined lines of fair and foul, was already set up to fit inside a stadium of fans who could get much closer to the action than in a sport like cricket where the batters needed as much space behind them as in front of them. Moreover, just as baseball was a good fit for middle-class players who could spend several hours after work in a game, the condensed nature of games appealed to middle-class fans who could afford to spend a little money and time on leisurely entertainment, but not too much. And just as playing baseball helped form communities among players who came from similar class positions, it allowed spectators of the middle class to gather together in support of regional teams, city teams, and so forth, in a way that fostered identification with other fans. Owners were able to translate the sociability inherent in playing baseball to the sociability of watching baseball, something that couldn't happen in cricket because it was too bound up in notions of exclusion rather than inclusion.

While middle-class citizens were the ones overtly courted to attend baseball games, most owners also felt as if their team had a moral and social obligation to society. Consequently, they often spoke of trying to rise above a "beer and whiskey" mentality, a phrase which grew out of the fact that many ballclubs in the late 19th century prohibited the sale of alcohol at the game so as to discourage drinkers—who were usually labeled "lower class"—from attending (Burk 69). In some ways, this functioned as a form of improving and educating the masses, encouraging the adoption of middle-class values through participation as a baseball fan. In doing so, baseball promoted the development of a middle-class character as fans gathered together and associated with masses of people coming from similar economic backgrounds and with similar interests, interests coincidentally also shared by the owners of the clubs. In short, baseball helped define how people understood middle-class America. In doing so, of course, it also recognized, as the century moved closer to 1900, the serious class tensions present in American life, as clashes over issues of class and status underscored baseball's social significance. As my introductory musings on the contrasts between cricket and baseball make clear, from the beginnings of their antebellum clash to baseball's clear victory as the century wound down, the sporting world was a world of class tension, as upper-class citizens struggled with the growing, coalescing middle class for the right to say what could be defined as "American."

BASEBALL AND SPORTS

Such would be the state of the ball-playing world when, in 1906, the young, fictional Jimmy Gatz scrawled a regimented schedule for himself that set aside time for morning exercises, study, work, elocution, and the like. When Gatsby's father produces the written record of this schedule inside a copy of *Hopalong Cassidy* during a conversation with Nick following Gatsby's death, he provides his own analysis of this schedule. His father's statements shed some light on the significance of this textual object, especially in terms of middle-class definitions of the American character. The schedule and general resolves which follow, and which Gatsby's father simply "came upon," are Mr. Gatz's only textual evidence for his claim that "[i]f he'd of lived he'd of been a great man. . . . He'd of helped build up the country" (131). As a small yet integral part of this to-do list, little Jimmy set aside a half hour every day for "baseball and sports" (135). The implication in the phrase "baseball and sports" initially sets baseball apart, as if it were not merely a sport, but something more—as if there were a greater weight imported to this activity than to other sports. In fact, in a small, mid-western town, baseball would have been considered something more. Jimmy Gatz's phrase "baseball and sports" as a part of a daily regimen speaks to the cultural narratives concerning the spread of baseball throughout the middle classes in the early part of the century. Young boys who would have actually followed such a schedule would have grown up to be the critical mass of "American" baseball fans migrating to the cities and filling the ballparks twenty years later, seeking out other fans with similar historical selves, working together to help "build up the country" according to their own set of social values and democratic ideals.

Major league baseball commissioner Kennesaw Mountain Landis called American boys who were *not* playing baseball "under-privileged" (469), and called for a concerted effort to incorporate baseball as part of physical education programs in schools across the nation. Landis's rhetoric echoes Theodore Roosevelt's "The Value of an Athletic Training" and suggests that baseball not only fulfills a physical need, but a patriotic one as well; no young boy can be truly American without baseball. J.A. Butler stated this sentiment even more explicitly, claiming that the way to build up a corps of "true American youth" was to have a baseball team in "every town, every church, every Sunday school, every fraternal order, every industrial plant, and every neighborhood" (24). Baseball was even more an object of middle-class American narrative than the mass-paperback copy of the childhood adventure in which the schedule was originally scribbled. As such, baseball frames Gatsby's past. The Jimmy Gatz he attempts to leave behind is one of Butler's "true American youth"; he was a Jimmy who played baseball, he was a Jimmy of the middle class.

By portraying young Jimmy as a baseball player rather than a spectator, Fitzgerald assigns him a sense of agency, in that Jimmy desires to place himself at the center of the spectators' attentions. We might wonder if Jimmy's overt attempts to construct himself as a boy who plays "baseball and sports" is a form of performance similar that which we saw from the main characters in the short stories from chapter 3. Jimmy Gatz's schedule is certainly a construction of a social persona; it was Gatsby's first effort of self-definition, his first attempt to define his character as he wanted it seen. Significantly, there is no portrayal of young Jimmy actually playing baseball, just a narrative record of his thoughts. Whether or not Jimmy followed his schedule, or whether he even liked baseball, is irrelevant. For Jimmy to schedule baseball—separate from sports—as part of his day, and thus as part of his schedule, is a representation of his desire at a young age to posit himself as a member of a particular class.

Yet baseball as a sport—meaning that which baseball had come to represent—conflicted with Gatsby's aspirations. He ultimately strove to represent himself not as a product of mainstream America, but as part of the "orgastic future" which he thought could be found in "gleaming, dazzling parties" (*Gatsby* 140–41). Gatsby's efforts at modeling rely upon a spectacle much different from that of a day at the baseball park; they require an illusion of upper-class culture. The fantasy which Gatsby sought after was unachievable through monetary accumulation alone, and hence he sought after representational signs of being upper class. As a component of this splendor, the "baseball" which little Jimmy Gatz played is, later in life, necessarily replaced by the photograph which he displays to Nick of Gatsby all decked out in his cricket uniform. The image which Gatsby presents to Nick for review uses a visual representation of cricket, along with the associations of British privilege and elitism that had been associated with that game for seventy five years in America, to rebuild himself as a member of a new class.

Ironically, while Gatsby uses the cricket picture to first align himself with a sense of British status and tradition, in some ways that picture also makes Gatsby appear more American—or at least, the type of American which he is trying to emulate through his accumulation of cultural signs. Gatsby is attempting to become one of the upper-class Americans who traces his social heritage to the "old sport"s of European blood. As Peter Mallios writes,

In Nick's mind at the time, it is unclear whether Gatsby's background is one of fine 'breeding' and a fine family like Nick's own, or something outside. Yet here . . . Gatsby becomes strikingly alive to Nick, becomes "truly" American to Nick, because he can flash experiential credentials that identify him with the former category.(382)

What the text seems aware of through these two vignettes, then, goes beyond a mere tension existing between the two sports. A baseball bat, while perfectly acceptable as the instrument of play for millions of young boys, couldn't provide the social position to a figure composing himself to be a member of a higher American caste. Of course, Jimmy Gatz's schedule is no less a cultural sign than the Oxford photograph. As Jimmy, he constructs a persona of the average, middle-western, middle-class boy; as Gatsby, he constructs himself to be the elite American cricket player. He invents his own story, casting off the sport that was supposedly born in America for one that was born of privilege and status. In both cases, however, Gatsby has constructed a self that is based on metonymic representation, using sport to build himself up just as that sport could "build up the country." In other words, Gatsby is the country, and he narrates his history through the symbols provided by the narratives of baseball and cricket, respectively.

Moreover, the juxtaposition of these two symbols of Gatsby's past identifies him, a *nouveau riche* figure who doesn't quite fit into either category, as precisely the site of the American class tension of the twenties (see Mallios 367, Berman 59–61). Gatsby assumes that the sign of high culture can overcome his reality, yet the cricket bat no more replaces his youthful baseball days than does his ostentatious wardrobe or décor, imported from England but modeled after the so-called "taste" defined, ironically, not by what the upper class wore but by what the mass-culture catalogs and media portrayed the upper class as wearing. As Richard Butsch writes, industries of leisure "encourage[ed] consumers' identification with the upper class and its luxury in an effort to promote consumption as a value. The entertainment industries in particular appealed to middle-class aspirations toward upward mobility" (16). Such mass culture representations of wealth and privilege, of which cricket is one of the primary examples, threatens to collapse the clear separation between the upper class and the middle class. Class itself becomes an issue of "style" (in relation to Gatsby's clothes and parties) or an issue of "play" (in relation to his cricket posing), either concept complicating the assumptions of classes as stable economic categories and clearly undermining any notion that class, even when demonstrated by physical, athletic sport, has a natural foundation.

CREATING BASEBALL'S ANCESTRY: WHITMAN, SPALDING, AND "MIDDLE-CLASS VALUES"

While I earlier mentioned several demonstrable features about baseball that made it more popular than other team sports among (first) players and (later) spectators, in calling it a middle-class American phenomenon I also recognize that a romanticism has historically surrounded baseball's supposed ability to exemplify middle-class values, a romanticism which Fitzgerald both desired and criticized. Towards the end of the nineteenth century and into the twentieth century, owners of professional teams continued to use ideologies of morality, social class, and community status as a way to sell tickets. At the same time, analyses of baseball as a social sport often focused on abstract descriptions of how baseball ideologically fit some concept of a "sensibility" belonging to a middle-class American type. It was already common to hear of baseball labeled as a "national pastime"[4]; Michael Novak notes how the late nineteenth century saw baseball fitting into philosophies inextricably connected to America's history. He finds records of statements that baseball was "born out of the enlightenment and the philosophies so beloved of Jefferson, Madison, and Hamilton," theories of baseball being a "Lockean game, a kind of contract theory in ritual form," and comments on the physical layout of players on a field being "designed as geometrically as the city of Washington" to baseball (58). This nostalgic romanticism of "self-evident" truths was by no means unique to cultural critics; one of the most well-known statements about baseball as a national game comes from Walt Whitman. In *With Walt Whitman in Camden*, Whitman is quoted as saying about the game: "it's our game: that's the chief fact in connection with it: America's game: has the snap, go, fling of the American atmosphere" (qtd. in Traubel 508). Whitman's claims about baseball go beyond the relationship between baseball and local middle-class communities. His rhetoric pushes past city clubs and neighborhood leagues, and associates baseball with the national community, specifically postulating a connection between baseball and what he calls an "American atmosphere." Under Whitman's logic, baseball belongs in the American historical landscape because the "atmosphere," another way of theorizing about the existence of a typical American lifestyle or even a typical American character, was amenable to the pace, style, and organization of the game.

At another time, Whitman made much the same statement, claiming:

> Base-ball is our game: the American game: I connect it with our national character. Sports take people out of doors, get them filled with oxygen—generate some of the brutal customs . . . we are some ways

a dyspeptic, nervous set: anything which will repair such losses may be regarded as a blessing to the race. (qtd. in Traubel 330)

For Whitman, baseball was a cultural possession of the American nation. He designates America as a having a particular "race," a race needing "repair" that baseball could provide. By espousing the notion that baseball is a sport belonging to America, and that baseball has helped to form America—or, in this case, re-form America following the Civil War—Whitman argues that baseball represents America, symbolically and literally. At least, it represents the America which Whitman himself envisioned. Ed Folsom, in analyzing this passage, argues that Whitman saw that baseball

> as a repairer of physical losses, a blessing to the race, and a gauge of national character, was one activity that helped Whitman bring together his persistent concerns with health, American originality. And preservation of the union . . . the sport was also one thing America could claim as its *own*. (42)

In other words, Folsom sees Whitman's logic as a claim that America needed baseball in order to stake a claim in a sense of exceptionalism; to be a nation required having a unique national sport, one superior to other sports and worthy of the national character, and baseball filled the void in a way that other sports—namely, cricket—could not.

Whitman elaborates on his argument for America's need to own baseball by claiming that the game "belongs as much to our institutions, fits into them as significantly as our constitutions, laws: is just as important in the sum total of our historic life" (qtd. in Traubel 508). By mentioning constitutions and laws, the governing rules of the nation, Whitman postulates that baseball is principally founded upon a democratic ideal. As one of America's "institutions," baseball inherits that part of the American atmosphere championing a sense of cultural democracy as well, at least in principle. Or, as Bill Brown argues, the idea of baseball being a "mode of fantasizing supposedly American traits" is one of the primary examples of "play being appropriated . . . as modes of reimagining the nation" (10–11).

Whitman's idealizations of the game of baseball rely upon a perception of the game, and of the nation, which often doesn't correspond with historical observation or close, analytical criticism. Rhetoric such as that espoused by Whitman is significant specifically in its connection to a particular historical figure, one of the many people on whom sport historians have bestowed the title, "Father of Baseball." The success of National League founding father A. G. Spalding came in creating a monopoly on professional baseball. He owed his monopoly in large part to the fact that he entered his business with a coherent picture of the type of crowd he felt baseball was suited for; The National League had been overtly courting a respectable, middle-class spectator base for 15 years, enforcing its desire for a certain type of fan by banning Sunday play, barring alcohol sales and gambling, and, most importantly, charging 50 cents for a ticket, a price out of the reach of poorer, lower-class laborers. More importantly, he comprehended the role that the audience was beginning to play in the game. He saw that successful baseball was much larger than the already old debate about the division between player and owner; the spectator was the motivating factor behind both. Spalding saw in the American middle-class spectator a desire to participate in the game yet still keep a sharp distinction between those on the field and those in the stands. Prior to the rise of baseball, the concept of spectator sport didn't always have such a clear delineation. According to Gorn, "the line between spectators and participants [in American sports] was thin; the man cheering one heat of a quarter-horse race might be riding in the next" (4). Consequently, Spalding tried to create a game that would appeal to this notion of a separate body of "participators" in the sport. The playing area already demarcated fair and foul territory, and as stadiums became more common than mere fields, owners or clubs had constructed grandstands and bleachers surrounding the field on all sides but set back from the playing grass a certain distance. Spalding's stadium was a step further, bringing the fans as close as possible to the action yet always clearly marking the architecture of the spectator space with walls, poles, and even pavilions and tents.

His choice to control the space of his crowds worked together with his keen understanding of who his crowd was, and he knew he could quantify his profits by pursuing a single community of fans. The developing economic and cultural power needed in order to provide such a community could be found only in a population which would possess enough time and money to spend on an afternoon at the ballpark. That games were played in the afternoon until the advent of lighted stadiums[5] is significant in setting baseball apart as a different form of leisure activity. Movies and vaudeville could take place in indoor, lighted theaters, allowing them to take place not only at night but also year round. But baseball could only be played during the day and only in good weather; thus the demographics of the crowd were even more limited. The lengthy workdays of the lower, working classes often prevented them from being able to visit the ballpark for a couple of hours during the middle of the day. Baseball, at the turn of the century, needed the middle class as much as it helped to create it.

While preserving the division between spectator and player, Spalding, as well as other owners in the National League, also understood the essential identification that needed to develop between a spectator and a team. Baseball clubs needed to have fans, not just attendees. The final quarter of the 19th century saw the development of such "innovations" as fixed schedules and home ballparks. Having a home team provided an incentive for the citizens of a given city to attend the games; it allowed them to feel a sense of investment and ownership over the players and to have a sense of security in the stadium and team as permanent objects in their urban landscape. Moreover, team nicknames—which had long been applied to different teams by newspapers—were adopted by the clubs themselves in hopes to take on an identity, an identity often linked to the identity of the fans. Noel Hynd reports, for example, that Jim Mutrie, manager of the New York club of the 1880s, officially labeled his club the Giants after seeing the reaction he got from fans for running through the crowd during a game exhorting "we, the people" to rally around "our boys, our giants!" (64). Often cultural critics today seek to locate the mythic roots of baseball in a rural, pastoral countryside, but the game literally grew out of middle-class urban centers, cities with large populations desirous to unite with the team and, importantly, with each other, in rivalry with other major cities. Thus Spalding's monopoly helped foster the notion that a typical day game was no longer just the Chicago club visiting the New York club, but was "their stinkin' Cubs" battling "our beloved Giants."

Spalding, in keeping with his major aim of monopolizing the business of baseball, saw that once he nurtured a solid core of a middle-class fan base, his next step was, in line with the nationalistic rhetoric already abounding in assessments of the sport, to connect baseball with a sense of Americanness. Americans, now in the wake of yet another war, this time the Spanish-American War, were once again becoming more and more invested in ideologies of nationalism and American exceptionalism and were eager to participate in things that were exclusively American. Spalding had already helped baseball become middle-class, and used middle-class desires for American uniqueness to solidify his baseball as the national pastime. As a marketing strategy for selling a line of baseball sporting goods,[6] Spalding voiced his opinion that "Americans are evolving into a fresh-air people. They are being converted to the gospel of exercise" (qtd. in Levine 83), rhetoric once again reminiscent of Theodore Roosevelt's strenuous life, implying that good athleticism equals good Americanism. By insinuation, then, baseball players are good Americans, and those who watch baseball—a population Spalding himself molded to be middle class in nature—are helping to build up the nation.

The French sociologist Bourdieu has recognized a historical connection between cultural class tension and sport. Tracing the emergence of "sports in the strict sense," Bourdieu notes that class "defines the meaning conferred on sporting activity, the profits expected from it" (qtd. in Sugden and Tomlinson, 318). In other words, participation in sport is not exclusively a matter of preference or taste. Instead, participation is largely governed by economic means and, more importantly, social expectations. Bourdieu also focuses on the "profits" that a given sport provides as a motivating factor behind sport; drawing from Weber's discussion of how status differs from class (which I touched on in the introduction), Bourdieu notes that certain sports have different cultural effects due to the expectations and desires of those playing or watching (319). He thus effectively argues that tennis, golf, and sailing, as individualized sports that bestow "gains in distinction" and honor a notion of leisurely amateurism, make up "an ethos which is that of the dominant fractions of the dominant class" (318). Baseball, on the other hand, a sport of middle-class participation and fanship, developed "in the form of spectacles produced for the people . . . more clearly as a mass commodity" (318). Given Bourdieu's statement, sport becomes an ideological tool, linking class standing to social character.

More intriguingly, in 1908 Spalding set up a commission to research the origin of baseball. Spalding's commission was nothing more than a thinly veiled method of constructing an American mythos of baseball; the commission reported that "Baseball was invented in 1839 at Cooperstown, NY by Abner Doubleday—afterward General Doubleday, a hero of the battle of Gettysburg—and the foundation of this invention was an American children's game called one old cat" (301). Spalding wanted an American history for his sport, so that faith in American exceptionalism could easily translate into faith in baseball's exceptionalism. Spalding needed a story of baseball, a narrative that would not contain overt traces of class-inflection or cultural manipulation but which would, instead, tell the tale of an American sport. To this end, and perhaps with Whitman in his cultural memory, Spalding decided that an American hero—a Civil War general who fought for the north, thus helping preserve the union—would be the game's father. Spalding's claims were soon repudiated, but historical fact did not release the hold that the myth of an American-born game had over the middle-class fans filling the grandstands.[7]

Spalding's value system and beliefs about baseball, class, and the nation are summed up in his response to the conflicts between the leagues; he declared that "when the spring comes and the grass is green upon the last resting place of anarchy, the national agreement will rise again in all its weight, and restore to America in all its purity its national pastime—the great game of baseball" (qtd. in Ward 40). The grass, of course, is a dual reference. His language echoes images of the civil war battlefields, specifically the Gettysburg hills where Doubleday helped lead the ultimate Union victory. At the same time, Spalding also brings to mind the baseball field, which is most definitely not a pastoral setting as many often argue. Instead, Spalding turns the image into an aggressive one, not necessarily in the sense of physical aggression but of cultural. The image of an open field of green grass subduing anarchy calls to mind the supposed economic and social progression of constructing a baseball stadium in an urban environment, taming the frantic landscape with an architectural entity housing a game of leisure and of middle-class taste. The construction of baseball stadiums within cityscapes was in part connected to the American park movement, where landscape architects such as Frederick Law Olmstead saw parks and gardens as a way to provide spaces of escape, spaces of health, and spaces of serenity within the vast expanses of the late-nineteenth century city[8]; At the same time, reading Spalding's statement as a description of a baseball park also charges the image with sentiments of American imperialism, playing into a conception of a pure "American" race needing to colonize in the name of democracy.

The duality of the metaphor pushes for a relationship between the two levels of significance, as if the stadium—what Ben Lisle calls the "middle-class paradise" (6)—is the path to true "Americanism." Spalding, focusing on making baseball economically successful, marketed the game as an American spectacle, tailor-made for the middle class striving to make *everything* more American. In doing so, he made baseball a locus of both communal and national class tension. Those that could possess the game of baseball (speaking ideologically) would, by extension, own its spectators, and thus possess America in the sense of steering social agendas that baseball had a stake in. Spalding wanted baseball to, in effect, colonize[9] America in the name of the middle class, while still inviting the spectators to think that they "owned" the team.

"WE'RE GOING TO THE BASEBALL GAME"

Just as we've seen Fitzgerald's examinations into the too-easily accepted promises of egalitarian opportunity and social mobility challenge how sport supposedly functions in American society, his treatment of baseball in *The Great Gatsby* provides a similar critique of the nostalgic, romantic assessment of the sport in relationship to the nation. Fitzgerald understood the solid relationships between the sport and the middle class; rather than making the leap from that relationship to idealistic rhetoric of baseball as a sign of American middle-class sensibility, however, Fitzgerald instead uses the sport to scrutinize the larger notion of "Americanness" as a tool for middle-class social structuring.

With Spalding "making" the game a middle-class experience in order to cater to the already prevalent nostalgia and romanticism surrounding baseball, the game in the 1920s—often called the golden decade of sport—only continued to express the notion that baseball symbolized some sort of intangible sense of Americanness. In doing so, the history of the class tensions surrounding the clashes between baseball and cricket, or perhaps more accurately the recognition of class difference between those involved in baseball and those involved in other sports, was largely glossed over. Sportswriters spoke of the ballpark as a place where, as a scholar in the *American Journal of Sociology* describes, "crowds of every background touch shoulders . . . laying aside differentials of rank" (qtd. in Seymour 11). Grantland Rice, perhaps the most heralded sportswriter of the decade, called baseball "he true democracy in the United States . . . [one] not to be found among our politicians, our so-called statesmen, our labor union leaders or our capitalists" (qtd. in Inabinett 17). The Spalding Commission, relying upon such paeanic prose, resulted in a strong, widely held belief in the myth of baseball as a natural and lasting symbol of democracy, an irresistible combination in post-war America. Fitzgerald,[10] to a small degree, was attracted to this myth of baseball as the foremost example of, to use his words, "the formless grace of our nervous, sporadic games" which makes Gatsby (in Nick's eyes) and baseball (in Spalding's eyes) "so peculiarly American" (51). Yet he also sees complexities that he attempts to work through in his use of baseball. Ultimately, by examining the baseball allusions in *The Great Gatsby* in conversation with Spalding's version of the narrative of the game, we can see how Fitzgerald posits baseball as not representative of the American middle class, but as representative of his larger assessment of the "American Dream"; baseball is a democratic chance at mobility that is moving away too quickly to ever secure.

The episodes which form chapter seven of *The Great Gatsby*—from the hot morning in the Buchanans' home, through the confrontation in the Plaza Hotel, to the death of Myrtle Wilson—are the climactic encounters of the novel and accentuate nearly every theme put forth in the novel. As such, the writing (and constant rewriting) of this section was the most troubling to Fitzgerald (Bruccoli 18). This portion of the text underwent the most radical changes from the typescript to the galleys to the revised galley proofs, with Fitzgerald making some emendations just days before the book went to press. While reviewing the page proofs, a process normally reserved for minor alterations or corrections, Fitzgerald added, deleted, and rewrote entire pages, even chapters of the text. Before these galley revisions, the manuscript had two versions of the pivotal scene; one familiarly takes place in a room at the Plaza Hotel, while the second, the rejected version, takes place instead at a baseball stadium (watching the visiting Chicago Cubs battle the local New York Giants) and includes a stop at an outdoor café in Central Park. This second version was completely excised by Fitzgerald during his galley revisions. Yet the text of this deleted passage, as well as Fitzgerald's eventual decision to remove it, works together with the few other allusions to baseball in the novel to demonstrate the degree to which baseball, in opposition to the idealistic rhetoric of the game's "democracy," in actuality reflected the class tension existing between middle-class and upper-class America. More specifically, the deleted text establishes the spectacle of baseball—the act of watching a game—as a microcosm for the national struggle between classes over cultural rights to define the national character.[11]

In the original manuscript, as in the published text, the Buchanans, Nick, Jordan, and Gatsby are driving from East Egg to Manhattan for the day and they pull over just before the bridge to discuss where they are headed. However, whereas in the published version the cars merely pull alongside one another and then continue driving to the Plaza Hotel, in the alternate manuscript version Tom parks the car and steps out, walking back to speak with Daisy and Gatsby. "This looks like a row to me," Jordan comments (Manuscript 180).[12] Upon his return to the car, he tells Nick and Jordan, tersely, "We're going to the baseball game" (180). The party then crosses the bridge, "split[ting] the city heat northward toward the polo grounds" (181). Rather than sitting in a private suite that "was large and stifling" (*Gatsby* 98), the setting for the published version, the alternate manuscript scene eschews passive consumption of space and instead literally drives the plot toward a location that is open and public. By placing the scene originally in a baseball stadium, the text first of all delivers a strong initial impression of a typical middle-class spectatorship. The crowd is one of mass culture consumption; Nick comments that "the smell of peanuts and hot butter and cigarettes mingled agreeably in the air" (Manuscript 182). This is the ballpark experience as it had evolved throughout the years, the park of Jack Norworth's melodic "Take Me Out to the Ballgame" (which was already a baseball relic by the 1920s). The emphasis on the crowd sets the scene as one of spectatorship, not one of athletic ability. Nick doesn't truly watch the game, but observes the crowd and makes note of it; the crowd is what dominates Nick's mind when he reveals to the reader that he "enjoyed that day" (182).

As the deleted scene continues, the crowd already at the game before the Gatsby party arrives is for the most part faceless, in that there is no real distinctive description of individual character. Instead, there is the body of the crowd. This holds true throughout the scene, with two exceptions; yet it is these two characters, those who receive special narrative attention, who provide Fitzgerald a critique of the assembly of middle-class spectators. These two characters are in some degree a representation of the marginalized "lower class," those that were excluded from the crowds that were supposedly supposed to be so inclusive of anyone willing to spend the day at the ballpark. First, behind the grandstands before entering the park, Jordan and Nick meet a little boy hoping to attend the game: "If she would only give him fifty cents, the little boy explained, he could get in and see the game" (182). The boy's desire to get into the park, perhaps some form of the middle-class desire, is to become part of the crowd. His goal is to unite with a mass body; he also wishes for social mobility. And while the ticket is only fifty cents, to him the money represents power. In his wish to join with the rest of the fans in watching the game from the inside, the little boy, much as Gatsby, sees money as an object of mobility and a means for achieving an intriguing mixture of acceptance, pleasure, entertainment.

The second figure belying the supposed egalitarian crowd is an unruly fan, someone who is "thrown violently from the bleachers for being drunk or sober or wrong" (182–83). Nick's assessment of this man underscores the class implications. Nick doesn't know what the fan has done, but it must have been "wrong"; he must not have known how to act properly. The added significance, however, is that textually this particular fan somehow stands out; he is noticeable by the reader as an individual figure rather than being a part of the "wild roar [that] went up inside the ball park balanced [sic] swelling for a long time" (182). Between these two caricatures, then, Nick is able to observe the position that the middle class finds itself in; the aura of community is paradoxically undermined both through the little boy who still finds himself excluded from this world of middle-class spectatorship as well as through the fan who, despite his lack of understanding of the "codes" of behavior is the only one able to distinguish himself.

In addition to the (often lack of) description of the characters at the ballpark, the physical structure and physical space of the baseball stadium itself also plays into this idea of a middle-class crowd serving as the center of the pivotal occurrences of this narrative passage. The ballpark where the Giants played was named "The Polo Grounds," despite the fact that polo was never actually played at the Polo Grounds of the twenties and beyond. However, the name still bears a historicity in its relation to the upper-class pursuit of polo. The original Polo Grounds, built on the corner of 110th and Sixth Avenue in Manhattan, was a polo field up until 1886 when Giants owner John Day leased the grounds from rich socialite James Gordon Bennett, Jr. Whereas the polo field was tightly safeguarded against uninvited guests, Day transformed the field into a diamond and grandstands, where only a ticket-taker would stand between someone and the game. The construction of a field, with the grass placed below the level of the seats and surrounded by the grandstands, underscores the power that these middle-class fans had. As a mass body, the spectators very literally encircled the players and towered over them, thus metaphorically exerting their will over the course that the game would take.

By accentuating the crowd and the stadium as the pivotal facets of this baseball scene, the text in this alternate version thus casts the confrontation between Tom and Gatsby not as a private affair but a public performance. The arguments between Gatsby, Daisy, and Tom work together with the action of the game on the field, and the confrontation between Tom and Gatsby in essence becomes a game itself played for a Daisy trophy before a mass of fans, eager to cheer on one side or the other. Existing in the public crowd, the altercation can be read as a popular, open forum, pushing the boundaries of the conversation subjects beyond a sphere of upper-class closed doors and into the space of public review, all represented by textually situating the episode within a baseball stadium.

As the manuscript text progresses, it continues to associate itself with the tensions involved in supposedly seeing baseball as a game of middle-class desires, making a logical leap from a notion of middle class that arises from the crowd to a sense of supposed democratic values which such a crowd embodies. While the two characters mentioned earlier represented the excluded lower class, the presence of Gatsby's party, and the conversations they have while at the game, are the other end of the spectrum; the text interrogates the class anxiety represented by the class divisions between Tom, Gatsby, and the middle-class crowd. "The Chicago Cubs were the visiting team" and, ironically loyal to his Midwestern roots, Tom "applauded with perfunctory patriotism" (183) while watching the Cubs in the field or at the plate. The geopolitical dynamics of baseball teams in the twenties are significant; the Cubs, although based in Chicago and thus seemingly representative of a Midwestern middle-class spirit, were actually more aligned with a sense of elitism within the baseball world. They were considered the first true dynasty of professional baseball (Golenbock 99, 155). Originally known as the White Stockings, the Cubs were one of the charter members of the National League in 1876. Albert Spalding was the longtime president of the

White Stockings, and his ideas of team organization, league relationships, and player/owner relations were often associated with the Chicago baseball club as a whole. The Cubs would, for America in the early twenties, represent tradition, history, and prestige.

In stark contrast, the New York Giants had no stable history as the Cubs did. They had been the National League New York Gothams in 1883–84, and became the Giants in 1885. When the Players' League (a rival project to Spalding's National League) collapsed, the National League Giants absorbed players from the upstart league who had shown promise in competition. Throughout the twentieth century, the New York Giants had been traditionally successful during the regular season. Yet they were still not considered a dynasty in the way that the Chicago Cubs were, given their lack of success in winning championships, at one point having lost four straight World Series. Because of this, the New York Giants did not generally command the attention from the media that the Cubs did; Chicago's success as national champions were often considered more representative of what baseball was about.

Yet at the time when the *Gatsby* crowd would be attending the game, the Giants would have been the reigning World Series champions, having won their first national championship in the fall of 1921. In fact, the Giants would also be the World Series victors in 1922; thus the Giants would represent the up-and-coming, the "new kids on the block" who show a world of promise in climbing the ladder of success. Because of their relative newness, their historical emphasis on the strength of the players, and their hometown appeal to the urbanites of Manhattan, they were widely heralded (along with the Yankees) as the team of the people. Their manager, irascible John McGraw, embodied this "self-made" spirit. His was a middle-class team with aspiring dreams, working to succeed on current effort instead of relying on what had been done in the past. McGraw himself saw his managerial style as one that emphasized a story of success based on effort and work rather than on natural endowment or talent; in an interview for *The Literary Digest* McGraw responded that

> When I broke into the game roughly thirty years ago I was considered a freak. Ball-players at that time were selected much as football-players are now, for their size. Unless a man was a six-footer and husky to boot, he wouldn't command much attention as a player. Size and weight were supposed to be necessary. . . . It was rather primitive reasoning. (96)

Implicitly, McGraw's language, in painting an image of himself as a small, "David"-like figure battling the goliaths of the baseball world, draws upon the narrative of the American success story. McGraw places himself in the position of newcomer, "one of those who drove" out "the old type of ball-player" (96). As manager of the Giants in 1921 and 1922, then, McGraw applied his characterization of himself to his team. The Giants, having finally captured a professional championship after years of narrow misses, could be considered an agent of the American success narrative just as McGraw was, overcoming adversity and conquering obstacles of position and history. The Giants were thus, to the crowd, a team of promise rather than a team of heritage; they were a team gaining popularity supposedly based on performance and work instead of on privilege and elitism.

Tom's partisanship toward the Cubs may likewise be read as an allegiance to a sense of empire and tradition as opposed to the "new kid" stance that was often applied to the Giants. With the Cubs representing Tom in this rubric, the Giants would then function as a symbol for Gatsby, as they have been breaking into a society doing everything possible to exclude them. Tom also demonstrates his sense of privileged taste, preferring finesse and purity in the game. Tom is drawn to fundamental baseball, favoring solid hits and solid defense rather than the flashy and powerful home-run hitting that was becoming en vogue through stars such as Babe Ruth. His applause comes "whenever [the Cubs] hit safely or pulled off a good play" (183). He clearly knows a lot about the game, yet even so his enthusiasm—coded as "patriotism"—towards the Cubs is only rendered as "perfunctory," as if he is performing to the requirements of his station (183). For Tom to become too involved with the game would still be beneath him. The Cubs may be analogous to his own conception of his social position, but the game itself was still a game of the masses. Tom's actions separate him from the fan whom Nick witnessed being thrown violently from the bleachers. As Tom structures behavior and performance, he is right, while the fan, as Nick recognizes, would be "wrong."

HERDING US INTO THAT ROOM

In the revised, published version of the novel, before entering the Plaza Hotel Nick mentions that "the prolonged and tumultuous argument that ended by herding us into that room eludes [him]" (*Gatsby* 98). The precursor to this "argument" is preserved in the final lines of the deleted passage at hand. Tom, with all his obligatory devotion to the Cubs, continues through most of the game in such manner, "[b]ut when he urged Daisy to do likewise she answered that she and Gatsby were for New York—after that he took no interest in the game" (Manuscript 183). That his wife would offer her allegiance to the

Giants rather than the Cubs was comparable to abandoning her position—a subtle declaration that she and Gatsby, despite Gatsby's own anxiety over his position, were assuming a personal future exclusive of Tom's status, wealth, and tradition. This personal future, by being coded through the language of baseball club allegiance, demonstrates the class tension involved here. Daisy's alignment with the Giants/Gatsby is an eschewal of old tradition, of Tom's sense of refined or elite taste and position. Moreover, baseball club allegiance becomes a type of nationalism, in the sense that Daisy is aligning herself with those whom she has never met and has nothing in common with except a shared ideology, in this case an abhorrence of the Chicago Cubs—or, more accurately, that which the Chicago Cubs represent for Tom.

The passage ends by hearkening back to its beginning, conspicuously conscious of the crowd of spectators: "Somebody won and we swept out with the crowd into the late afternoon" (Manuscript 183). The game was not about the final outcome, but about "the crowd." The baseball scene, framed between "the smell of peanuts and hot butter" and being "swept out with the crowd" underscores the vital nature of the spectatorship at the ballgame. Perhaps even more important in this discussion is Nick's choice of words and his narrative approach. As narrator, he provides no details throughout the passage—"someone" was thrown from the park, the pitcher is left unnamed, "somebody" won the game. Yet despite the ambiguity, despite not having concrete, specific memories that, for baseball, are not just important but of vital significance (baseball is a game of minutiae, of precise scorekeeping and incessant recording of detail), Nick still "enjoyed that afternoon." His enjoyment, therefore, rather than being located in that which normally makes a baseball fan—the players, teams winning, and so forth, is centered on what he has already included. The lack of detail and the emphasis on the crowd establishes the focus and power of the passage on the collective—images of mass bodies and communal activity—rather than the individual. The ultimate community event, the baseball game functions symbolic of the nation of the time, as an accumulation of people unified through shared experience. Significantly, the experience is one of middle-class consumption. Yet the communal consumption that the passage both starts and ends with, while the accepted and popular version of how baseball functions in a society, is undermined by the conspicuousness of the characters on both ends of the class spectrum, characters unable to be subsumed by mass culture consumption. The scene is as much about the incompatibility of the middle class with the upper class, as both sides see their own version of social life as taking precedence.

Of course, this analysis all hinges on a passage of text which Fitzgerald undeniably chose to excise from the published object. While significant as a textual object that we can read and analyze, this passage is even more significant in the fact that it *is* a deleted text. Bruccoli asserts that Fitzgerald "felt that he never managed to get Daisy's reaction exactly right" (*Apparatus* 18). The published text portrays a Daisy much more unsure about her decision to join with Gatsby; she ultimately remains with Tom, "retreat[ing] back into their money or their vast carelessness or whatever it was that kept them together" (*Gatsby* 139). The Daisy at the baseball game would not have been the same Daisy at the end of the novel, a wavering figure unable to discard the world that Tom provides for her. In fact, it can be assumed that precisely because of the mass culture spectacle that a baseball game was in the twenties, a figure such as Daisy (the Daisy as she is characterized throughout the rest of the novel) theoretically would never agree to attend such an event. Jordan Baker's golf matches might be allowed, perhaps, but a Giants game—that would be too middle-class given Daisy's refusal to relinquish her status in all other circumstances. Fitzgerald's act of textual excision represents not only his attempts to revise Daisy's reactions to the class-inflected tensions surrounding her character, but his recognition that, given such tensions, the class status which the Buchanans possess cannot exist in even a textual space of mass (and hence, for them, middle-class) culture.

Moreover, Fitzgerald's process of revision strengthens the argument that he understood how baseball was functioning in the American class structure; he understood the tense class friction involved in sport spectatorship and realized what it would mean to include the baseball passage in the novel. Fitzgerald's choice of the Plaza scene over the Polo Grounds produces not merely stylistic differences, but thematic ones. Fitzgerald himself is choosing the upper-class locale over the middle-class one. His revision relocates the climax from the public sphere into the private—the relationship between "upper-class" citizens such as Tom and Daisy, after all, is not a democratic one, nor is it one for public, mass presentation. This isn't to make the claim that class position entertains a one-to-one correspondence with space, but that the tension between public/private in this sense represents a certain amount of control and power, control and power essential for the maintenance of the Buchanans' upper-class status. For Tom to triumph would require a locale worthy of his class status—the tasteful Plaza Hotel instead of a "classless" (in this case, a word more signifying of homogenous class) day at the ballpark. In the Plaza Hotel, democracy and equality are not the dominant rule and Tom and Daisy are not signs of conspicuity, but are trademarks for their own version of social community, one of smelling mint Julep and listening to Mendelssohn rather than pursuing the things that the middle-class baseball fans do (*Gatsby* 98–99).

THE FAITH OF FIFTY MILLION PEOPLE

As the revision history of the novel is a subtext that innervates the climactic scene, Fitzgerald's portrayal of Jay Gatsby's past and present in *The Great Gatsby* is also bound up in baseball in one other way that is perhaps the most significant in the novel. Fitzgerald's deleted snapshots of a day at the ballpark reveal many of the underlying class tensions behind baseball's claim as "America's Sport," yet his focus on one of the most well-known historical baseball events, the 1919 World Series, thoroughly exposes the complexities and ironies in both the upper-class privileged life and in the middle-class dream for an equal opportunity. In doing so, the novel's central battle, the deep conflict between the middle class and the upper class, is culturally informed by the clash between over the issue of athletics and Americanism. More specifically, the novel produces an awareness that the narrative of baseball, both in history and in the myth which Spalding attached to the game, is at its heart the narrative of middle-class America.

While Gatsby struggles to overcome his baseball playing middle-class heritage, the man who recognizes him as a "fine appearing gentlemanly young man" and "made him" in business (133), Meyer Wolfshiem, is profiting from baseball the easy way. After meeting Wolfshiem and being "coolly" told by Gatsby that "he's the man who fixed the World's Series back in 1919,"[13] Nick's internal monologue narrates the significance of the historical event to his own perception of the masses involved as fans of the game: "It never occurred to me that one man could start to play with the faith of fifty million people—with the single-mindedness of a burglar blowing a safe" (78). Of course, initially the words "fifty million people" must be underscored—the World Series, perhaps the most important American sporting event at the time, represents not just the "best of baseball" but serves as the locus of spectatorship for early twentieth-century America. The baseball that these fifty million were watching was the culmination of the enterprise in which "owner-builders [were] interested in establishing their sport as the personification of middle-class values, which, at the time, were synonymous with morality, respectability, and civic-mindedness" (White 86). Though gambling on baseball was not illegal at the time, it was viewed as antithetical to the "spirit" of the sport (and by extension the spirit of the American citizen) inasmuch as it allowed for profit without work.

Hand in hand with gambling came cheating, and a historical figure such as Arnold Rothstein (on whom Fitzgerald's Meyer Wolfshiem was modeled) threatened not just the sport of baseball, but, metaphorically, American democracy. The foreman of the jury assigned to probe the scandal of the 1919 series claimed that "baseball is more than a national game, it is an American institution, [our great teacher of] respect for proper authority, self-confidence, fair-mindedness, quick judgment and self-control" (qtd. in Ward 142). For Meyer Wolfshiem to "play" with the faith stresses a middle-class nervousness about its own tenuous position in American society; if the sacred World Series could be fixed, then perhaps other cultural spaces or objects were just as vulnerable. Perhaps the promise of equality that democracy offered was at risk. Most importantly, perhaps the middle class was indeed powerless in the face of greater wealth than they could accumulate. If we consider our discussion from the last chapter about the staging of a ballgame as a social performance between fan and player, then the fact that a figure outside the spectator/idol relationship could fix the performance demonstrates that *neither* party "owns" the game. Hence, Nick's expressed astonishment is not just at the fact that a baseball game could be tampered with; Nick, in imagining the fifty million fans, sees middle-class American life in peril. Their desires for identification, their desires to have shared experience, their desires to further an egalitarian ideology, all are both corruptible and gullible. Garnishing an "unutterabl[e] awareness of our identity with this country" (*Gatsby* 137), Nick's reacts to Wolfshiem, ultimately, in a way that vocalizes the anxiety of the fifty million people whose class ideals baseball was supposed to represent.[14]

Wolfshiem's actions, exposing the apprehension of middle-class America, are a noteworthy correlative to another episode of corruptibility in sport, Jordan Baker's alleged cheating in a local golf tournament. Amateur golf, a sport policed not by on-site umpires as in baseball or other sports, is instead based completely in personal integrity. Players are responsible for their own scoring and submission of scorecards. Yet even with privilege in wealth, talent, and status, Jordan still feels compelled to attain an advantage over other competitors, in order to reap, in Bordieu's terms, social profit—the honor and status accorded to a champion of a golf tournament, a tournament sponsored by and paid for by the same country club members with whom she would be ingratiating herself. In this respect, then, Jordan Baker's action in altering the lie of her ball is perhaps more profound than Wolfshiem's involvement in throwing the World Series. Yet these two instances exhibit radically different conceptions of how citizens in competing classes function with associates. Jordan's deception ostensibly hurt "the spirit of the sport" and her fellow competitors, who would have been on the same class level as she. Yet Meyer Wolfshiem's connection to the World Series scandal can be figured not just as taking advantage of a sport or personal honor, but as economic exploitation of a lower class through the destruction of America's game. Wolfshiem fixing the World Series is an attempt to take baseball, and thus by extension take America, away from the middle class.

Wolfshiem's characterization is also important not just in terms of his wealth or class but in terms of his ethnicity. Wolfshiem is Jewish, almost excessively so. And while Fitzgerald's ethnic stereotyping of Wolfshiem has been called everything from sloppy satire to Nordic anti-Semitism,[15] what's interesting here is not *just* that Wolfshiem is Jewish, but that he is so visibly so. He is a thorough collection of Jewish stereotypes, from his thickly accented discussion of business "gonnections" (56) to the description of Wolfshiem's "expressive nose" (55). In fact, Nick's very first visual perception of Wolf-shiem characterizes him as a figure perhaps not quite human, but closer to an animal: "A small flat-nosed Jew raised his large head and regarded me with two fine growths of hair which luxuriated in either nostril. After a moment I discovered his tiny eyes in the half darkness" (55). Wolfshiem is so very overtly alien in a novel about the problems of trying to define "American." The fact, then, that this foreign character is the one able to fix the sport of the middle class only deepens the anxiety, for as Nick's expressions of worry about the ability to play with the faith of fifty million people expresses class anxiety, Wolfshiem's ethnicity extends that to a fear of racial degeneration. Baseball, the "American" sport, was tampered with by one so, according to the rhetoric of nativism that we saw in chapter two, un-American.

Ironically, Jewish-Americans have always traditionally had a very strong affinity for baseball, primarily as spectator. Eric Solomon writes that in the 1920s and 30s, the great pressure for immigrants to culturally assimilate made baseball, heralded as the national game, the focus of leisure for Jews wishing to emulate the dominant cultural activities (22). What's more, the intricate connection between history and mythology provided a structural familiarity to those undergoing a cultural transformation. According to Solo-mon, "baseball . . . was a substitute for the *shtetl*, a center of perception and community with strong cultural traditions, psychological sanctions, and emotional commitments, and the *shul*, a center of belief and ritual" (23). Per-haps Wolfshiem's fix, then, refutes this easy answer as to baseball's popularity among Jewish communities. Jewish immigrants felt that becoming baseball fans would help them become more American, yet Wolfshiem clearly had no such desire. Rather than give into the pressure to assimilate to American cul-ture, Wolfshiem subverts the power of assimilation, destabilizing one of the institutions that sought to nativize ethnic cultural practice.

There is another, more subtle significance to Nick's casual encoun-ter with Wolfshiem, an encounter which elicits these thoughts from Nick: "The idea staggered me. I remembered of course that the World's Series had been fixed in 1919 but if I had thought of it at all I would have thought of it as a thing that merely *happened,* the end of some inevitable chain" (78). As important as the phrase "fifty million people" is in understanding that which Wolfshiem's actions signify for the national class tensions in baseball, a more intriguing phrase is Nick's claim that if he had thought about it at all (implying that he hadn't thought about it at all), he would see it as the result of some "inevitable chain." Nick "assumes an absence of purposive agency" (Lauricella 87), as if a historical determinism had orchestrated the fix rather than a single person. Wolfshiem's individual actions are figured as collective ones, and his agency is thus subsumed by a cultural evolution. Such a concept places greater emphasis on the historical narratives of base-ball, the specific ones such as those at the beginning of this chapter as well as, significantly, the underlying mythic American narrative which Spalding created for the sport. By labeling the fix of the 1919 world series "inevitable," Nick makes a statement about the connection between baseball, class, and the nation; Spalding's narrative of a sport born in America, raised during the civil war and industrial revolution, and controlled as a middle-class spectacle in the twentieth century is a story with just one conclusion—Wolfshiem's fix. Such a logical progression not only removes Wolfshiem's agency, but his culpability as well. His attempts to take America away from the middle class expose the reality that middle-class life itself is responsible for the downfall of the sport they are trying to champion. In other words, by accepting the stories they do about baseball's exceptionalism and its embodiment of their version of American values, the middle class is powerless to effect a change in the inevitable chain.

With this conclusion, it is possible to read this particular passage about gambling in baseball as Nick's estimate of what the future of the country might be for the middle class. The image of the green island in the novel's final pages (*Gatsby* 140), representative of the cultural past from which Gatsby was trying to escape, is as inevitable as the fixing of the World Series. The middle class may cultivate "the last and greatest of all human dreams" (140)—dreams of success, wealth, and status; they may have a fascination of a land which prom-ised the prospects and opportunity for social mobility. But their hopes for "the new world"—that which they wanted the nation to be—are elusive, receding, and ultimately unreachable, despite placing their faith in things "peculiarly American." Or, given Meyer Wolfshiem's ability to play with faith, perhaps because of it. It would not be too much of a stretch to tease out a relationship between baseball and this final passage, the "green breast" of the new world and the "green light" at the end of Daisy's dock in some way correlating with Spalding's image of the grassy, green baseball field that he claims will subdue all anarchy. What *The Great Gatsby* says about baseball which Spalding could not understand is that to create one's own story, to rewrite history, begins the "inevitable chain" of failure. Gatsby "sprang from his Platonic conception of himself," something which baseball attempted to do as well. Gatsby failed. And if baseball represents middle-class America, then Nick, in looking at Meyer Wolfshiem and thinking of the inevitable chain that led to the fixing of the World Series, foreshadows the ways in which the "green breast of the new world" would be replaced by "the vast obscurity beyond the city, where the *dark fields* of the republic rolled on under the night" (141, emphasis added).

Fitzgerald's aims and aspirations may have been lofty; uncovering the complexities of a national identity and the associations between the nation and its mass body of people is perhaps a much too presumptuous goal. Yet presumptuous or not, Fitzgerald reveals some glaring truths about social disjunction in the national imaginary at the time. A detailed reading of the baseball allusions within *The Great Gatsby*, examining not just how but why baseball was so relevant in relation to the novel's aspiration to portray class tension of 1920s America, yields a better understanding of the anxious complexities of class relations and emerging nationalism during the tumultuous decade. Fitzgerald may have invited his readers to "imagine the confusion that Ring [Lardner] faced on coming out of the ball park" ("Ring" 37), but both within and without the text of *The Great Gatsby* he invites us to see the products of this confusion and to understand the power of an institution such as baseball in defining the roles and boundaries of those who claim to make up the American society.

Coda
Of Habitus and Homecoming

In the last chapter, I touched on the theories of Pierre Bourdieu as a way to discuss the ways in which sport provides a sort of social profit; people are motivated to participate in sport because of the rewards that it supposedly offers. While the rewards may be partially economic for those who partici- pate as player, they don't have to be, and in fact one of the major assertions I make throughout this entire book is that the social significance of sport is very often just as centered in Weber's notions of status. Moreover, my cen- tral point in chapter three about the social status bestowed through football performance exemplifies the argument that underscores all of my analysis: "success," athletic or otherwise, is a construct that only finds meaning within larger frameworks of social interaction. That is, there is nothing inherently significant about performing well in an athletic competition, nor does superi- ority within the bounds of a given game point to any natural sense of power, position, or community. Yet while not natural, the consequences of athletic ability are not any less real than other forms of power, and in fact the stories told about sport are in some ways much more powerful in their ability to perpetuate ideologies of status from one generation of athletes and spectators to another. The social capital, to return to Bourdieu's concept, which spec- tators bestow upon athletic stars or even sports themselves has historically fostered a perception of sport as a means of social mobility (and, connected with this, economic mobility), whether we talk about the rise to the top of a closed University system or about attempts to enrich one's class position within larger national formations.

Much of Bordieu's work relies upon an understanding of the term "habitus." Bourdieu calls habitus "a system of durable, transposable disposi- tions that functions as the generative basis of structured, objectively unified practices" (vii). In other words, habitus is a lens through which members of a younger generation perceive the cultural practices and attitudes of the preceding generation and leads to the reproduction of a social group. In each chapter, I discussed models of passing ideology from one generation to another through sport; these models of observation and emulation, whether in the form of witnessing national icons as they narrate their stories, striving to become a big man on campus by marching behind the football captain, playing the role of a hero in order to win the adoration of a crowd, or participating in a culturally subsuming myth of sport-based nationalism, can all be termed part of the habitus that structure the way that spectators relate to sport personalities. Habitus is in no way a determination of behavior, but rather a set of experiences and beliefs that mediate between perception and action (5.1). According to Laberge, Bourdieu's notion of habitus is one of the primary factors involved in social group formation, because it helps members of a group see common bonds that encourage them to behave in similar ways.

It is within this notion of habitus that ritual comes into play once again. While I have most completely discussed the rituals of sport performance and sport spectatorship in chapter three, notions of ritual are a subtext running throughout my entire argument and which, I put forth, form the basis of spectator's interactions with athletes. It is the ritual behavior of fanship which makes a fan a fan, which makes a star a star, and which makes a sport so much more than just a sport. Spectators form communities within sport glued together by the rituals of attending games at a stadium or holding tailgate parties, of sporting team colors and images of team mascots, of constructing fantasy leagues and collecting trading cards. These communities are more than just makeshift societies of convenience, but are microcosmic social systems that help explain larger conflicts of status and class lying outside of sport. This is why I take the effort to explore the communities of fans and players and the stories that have been perpetuated through sporting history. The impetus which fans feel for participating in the spectacle of sport, particularly its rituals, reveals the power that sport has in propagating ideologies of status from one generation to the next.

My research for part of this book led me to Princeton University on several occasions in order to access some of their libraries' special collections. In preparing for one of these trips, someone suggested that, while at Princeton, I ought to attend a football game, just so I had some visual images to accompany my historical and literary research. It was the middle of the college football season, and as I checked to see if Princeton would be in town the weekend, I couldn't believe my luck. Not only were they playing at home, but it would be Homecoming weekend. Even more exciting, the Homecoming game would be Princeton's annual battle with Yale.

Used to attending football games in the PAC-10 or the ACC, I was surprised when I arrived half an hour early and saw the stands more or less empty. Perhaps sport has lost any remaining Ivy League cachet, I reasoned. But over the next twenty minutes, dozens of massive groups of fans, having downed the last ounces of beer at whichever alumni tailgate party they had been invited to, filed in and quickly filled up row after row. It wasn't long, before this mass of fans became a cheering, screaming, stomping, community. At first I thought it was the football playing that was the cause of their enthusiasm; it quickly became clear to me, however, that they would cheer and yell at *any* play, well-executed or not.

The dynamics of this type of spectatorship fascinated me, and when my wife left to get something from the concession stand I took the chance to lean over and ask a few fans close by about their reasons for attending. The answers were all pretty much the same: "We've always done it," "All our friends attend," and "it's just part of being a Princeton graduate." In essence, I surmised, their attendance at the game, and their attempts to get involved in cheering and "supporting the team" as much as the student section might be expected to, was a social act. For them, it was not about the game on the field but about their interaction with their neighbors and fellow alumni. They had learned, undoubtedly from their own parents or friends who had attended Princeton, that going to the homecoming game was just something that was expected of them—it was part of the role of being a Princeton graduate. Their particular understanding of their social status was clear by their dress, and their attempts to maintain that status within their social circles was marked by their attendance and enthusiastic spectatorship. It was a ritual for them, repeated year after year.

To be honest, the analysis here in this book about the position of sport in society might be more difficult to apply to the contemporary Princeton football team. Undoubtedly, the members of the team still receive a form of social capital—campus-wide popularity, if you will—from having their names and "athletic photographs" splashed together in promotion flyers and game programs alongside stories and pictures of the Princeton greats—Snake Ames, Edgar Allan Poe,[1] Sunford White, and of course Hobey Baker. Yet today's Ivy League athletics have no where near the national presence that they did in the last part of the nineteenth and first part of the twentieth centuries. But in actuality, this ironically helps reinforce my argument that it is the institution of sport rather than the individual characters that exert social influence. For the fans at the alumni game, it was about the game itself— attending it, cheering at it, vicariously participating with the players on the field. It was about the community they had created, a community still using football as a means to identify with each other and to mark their own sense of exclusive, impenetrable social standing. I could never have participated in the type of fanship that I witnessed that day, because I did not have any means for garnering the status granted to Princeton alumni who attend the homecoming game year after year. I wasn't part of the "habitus," so to speak, and had no one from which to learn.

On the national level, where the social consequences of sport are most publicly realized today, there is still this habitus. Spectators still form communities, communities which find their meaning in participation and ritual. Relationships between player and national icon create levels of adoration which only serves to deepen the stories about sport as a means for social mobility. Yet for those trying to break into these relationships, to become today's equivalent of Fitzgerald's "Big Man," the stories quickly become unaccessible. Without Bourdieu's habitus, one cannot take part. I do not deny that talent somehow paradoxically plays a role, in that fans grant status to those players able to satisfy their idea of what a sport star should be. But this is not a phenomenon that lies within the agency of an individual player, any more than Amory Blaine, Bill the young football actor, or even the Great Gatsby himself could choose to cross a particular social boundary.

Ultimately, as sport continues to foster notions of stratification among players, among fans, and between the two groups, it creates hierarchies of status as well as class, hierarchies which Fitzgerald astutely identified in his own conversations with the narratives of sport. Today, Fitzgerald's observations, working together with what we can see about the state of contemporary institutions of sport and spectatorship, demonstrate that sport's ability to highlight, reaffirm, and reproduce the values of American society is a credible claim. Credible, that is, as long as we understand which American values we are really talking about.

Notes

NOTES TO CHAPTER ONE

1. My discussions of the early history of football that are not specifically cited are a compilation of commonly found information; especially helpful are Tom Perrin's *Football: A College History*, Mark Bernstein's *Football: The Ivy League Origins of an American Obsession*, and Walter Camp's *The Book of Foot-ball*.

2. Obviously, my assertions are based on a generalization that is not completely universal. It might be fruitful to consider stories that don't fit the mold or even work subversively; take Jack Johnson, for example, the African-American boxer in the 1910s and 1920s whose triumph over Jim Jeffries is usually framed in terms of a victory that threatened and destabilized the desires and ideologies of the racial and socioeconomic majority. For more discussion of Jack Johnson, see chapter 2.

3. Interestingly enough, Klein later makes the argument that one of the reasons there is a disproportionate ratio of Dominican major league players when compared to other nations is that in a country such as the Dominican Republic, baseball is both simultaneously a tool of hegemony *and* a tool of resistance; that is, because the sport, introduced from Cuba in the latter-half of the nineteenth century, has evolved under both American and Caribbean influences, the game itself is structurally different, a phenomenon which gives Dominican players athletic advantages over their American counterparts.

4. The other two athletes who made "Ofelia's" American Dream Team were Lou Gehrig, Yankee baseball player from the 30s who at one point played in 2,130 consecutive games and later succumbed to ALS (commonly known as "Lou Gehrig's Disease"), and Wilma Rudolph, an African-American track star who was physically handicapped due to a childhood case of scarlet fever, but who nevertheless won several medals in the 1956 and 1960 Olympic games.

TES TO CHAPTER TWO

1. Specifically, Camp is credited with the development of the controlled scrimmage, where the game is made up of a series of set downs, allowing teams a chance to plan their strategy and execute it one move at a time. The controlled scrimmage separates the game of American football from the fluid, uninterruptible movement in rugby or soccer (Powel 53).

2. Strictly speaking, there was no Ivy League, meaning an officially sanctioned association between the football clubs of the given schools, until the second half of the twentieth century. When I use the term "Ivy League" in this chapter, then, I am referring to the schools that would become the Ivy League, notably Harvard, Yale, and Princeton, as well as Columbia, Cornell, Dartmouth, Penn, and Brown. The term itself is as much a description of a cultural attitude as it is an enumeration of particular universities.

3. Tom Perrin notes that while the game was becoming popular in Midwestern universities as well, notably the University of Michigan, the University of Chicago, and the University of Notre Dame, it wasn't until the 1920s when Midwestern and Southern schools replaced the Ivy League as the national powerhouse institutions (32–34).

4. At least, this was his most verbal reason, although he had been held back a year for academic failure (due in part to extended illness) and was on the verge of expulsion for poor academic performance.

5. Spengler being the other.

6. This is a textual representation of an actual movement among Princeton students in 1917 who tried to create a great "University Hall" to replace the various aristocratic clubs. The movement, led by Richard Cleveland (the son of former President Grover Cleveland), saw many of the same problems in the club system that Woodrow Wilson had earlier identified. The revolt lost steam when the United States entered World War I.

7. For a complete discussion of the relationship between Princeton, Fitzgerald, and social Darwinism, see Bert Bender's "'His Mind Aglow': The Biological Undercurrent in Fitzgerald's *Gatsby* and other works."

8. For a discussion of the racism Jack Johnson faced and its cultural significance, see Gail Bederman's *Manliness and Civilization: A Cultural History of Gender and Race in the United States.* For a similar discussion of Jim Thorpe, see Jack Newcome's *The Best of the Athletic Boys: The White Man's Impact on Jim Thorpe.*

9. Interestingly, there is a specific moment in the text where sport is not conflated with other localized Princetonian social institutions, but with a national one that much of the Princeton culture appropriated—war. World War I became the event to which most Princeton students, especially athletes, turned as a sign of achieving significance on a larger level. Or, as the text puts it, "Every night the gymnasium echoed as platoon after platoon

swept over the floor and shuffled out the basketball markings" (139). A 1932 Princeton publication entitled *Princeton in the Great War*, which was given as a 25th anniversary gift to the Princeton class of 1917 (both Fitzgerald's and Amory's class) details the allure that many Princeton students saw in enlisting in the armed forces. Serving in the war was seen as perhaps a way to continue garnering status and accolades rather than toiling away, unknown, in a career after college. Hobey Baker became a fighter pilot, and when he crashed his plane and died just days before returning home, many wondered if it was not intentional, as if the thought of facing anonymity in the world was too much to handle after the glory-filled days of football and fighter planes.

In 1919, following news of Baker's death, the newspaper *Stars and Stripes* wrote that the loss added "another gold star in Princeton's athletic service flag," and went on to note that nineteen former Princeton athletes had died and another ten had been wounded in the war. The article concludes by stating that "upon this roll of honor are recorded many names that have only to be mentioned to recall to mind historic battles fought out upon the gridiron."

Messenger has read the passage detailing Amory's encounter with Allenby as a representation of war, with the "blue and crimson" colors of Yale and Harvard, which Allenby is promising to overrun, figurative of soldier's uniforms and blood. In Messenger's reading, the optimistic, orderly, Romantic phalanx stands in stark contrast to the later haunting image of the dead and mangled face of Dick Humbird.

In "The Crack-Up," Fitzgerald specifically equates not being good enough to play college football with not being able to get overseas to fight in World War I.

10. Pearl James offers an alternative reading of Amory's anxiety and its relation to sport, suggesting that sport functions not as a social or class-based response, but as a specifically masculine response to the anxiety caused by industrialization (3).

NOTES TO CHAPTER THREE

1. Mangum, for example, points to "Winter Dreams," "The Sensible Thing," "Absolution," and "Rich Boy," among others, as stories in which Fitzgerald worked through ideas of the American Dream and all its complexities, using such stories as a sort of laboratory for his writing of *The Great Gatsby* (68).

2. For example, Tom Buchanan in *The Great Gatsby* was a former Yale All-American, and Nick Carraway several times assesses Tom's behavior in terms of his college football days. Yet the short stories dealing with football written around the time of *Gatsby* do not visibly "workshop" a football-playing figure who would evolve into Tom. See the next chapter for a more in-depth discussion of Tom Buchanan as a former All-American Yale star.

3. The character of Frank Merriwell was revived for comic strips in the 1920s, for film in 1935, and for radio in the 1940s. The 1910s and 1920s also saw series based around Frank Merriwell's brother, Dick, and his son, Frank Jr.

4. Dime novels are usually defined as stories which appeared in actual book form; usually quite short and containing only one story, these novels proliferated throughout the end of the nineteenth century. Pulp magazines, on the other hand, began with *The Argosy* in 1896 (published by Frank Munsey as a companion to his more established periodical, *Munsey's Magazine*) and would publish weekly or monthly collections of stories from a variety of authors. Pulp magazines take their name from the pulp paper (paper cheaper and of a lower quality than the glossy paper used for the "slicks"—*The Saturday Evening Post*, for example) with which they were made.

5. Additionally, by choosing writing as his substitute for football in this passage, Fitzgerald is also saying something about the role that an author must play in terms of his social interaction, commenting on the way that an author is giving a performance in hopes of earning some sort of accolades much as the football hero does. See my analysis in this chapter of "'Send Me In, Coach'" for more discussion of the parallels between football hero as public performer and author as public performer.

6. Critics usually refer to Fitzgerald's years before publishing his first story in a commercial magazine as his apprentice years.

NOTES TO CHAPTER FOUR

1. The more general topic of "sports in *The Great Gatsby*" has been discussed critically, though not at great length. Richard Lessa's short article " 'Our Nervous, Sporadic Games': Sports in *The Great Gatsby*" discusses Fitzgerald's use of sport as "a principal means of delineating character," specifically looking at the portrayal of Tom Buchanan's college football days and Jordan Baker's golf career as a way of "bring[ing] out a trait or quality of an individual" (69). More specifically, John A. Lauricella has examined baseball in *The Great Gatsby* by arguing that Meyer Wolfshiem fixing the World Series is merely a convenient metaphoric setting for Fitzgerald to depict the thematic tension between innocence and "issues of duplicity and moral corruption" (88). Robert Johnson, Jr., in "Fitzgerald's Use of Baseball in *The Great Gatsby*, argues much the same thing, that the World Series scandal appears in the novel as an "enduring symbol . . . of the American Dream gone awry" (43). Yet none of these arguments sufficiently explore the relationship between baseball as a national symbol and the class tension surrounding the playing, and more importantly the watching, of the sport.

2. Incidentally, Fitzgerald had hoped to publish *The Great Gatsby* by the title *Under the Red, White, and Blue,* which perhaps would have provided a more overt reference to his attempts to understand the defining of an atmosphere

of American "values" through the novel. He was prevented from doing so only because he was tardy with a last-minute telegram.

3. For a more in-depth discussion of the relationship between the formation of early baseball conventions and the association with middle-class communities, see Tom Melville's *Early Baseball and the Rise of the National League.*

4. Baseball's claims to national significance were first legitimized when, in the 1860s, Andrew Johnson would host well-publicized games between the Washington Potomacs and the Washington Nationals on the makeshift field just south of the White House. See George Gipe's *The Great American Sports Book.*

5. The first night baseball game was played in 1935 between the Cincinnati Reds and the Philadelphia Phillies, a game in which Franklin Delano Roosevelt turned on the stadium lights from the White House.

6. Spalding, using his power as league president, set regulations on using certain types of baseballs, bats, and bases. He also introduced the use of baseball gloves, and soon mandated regulations on those as well. The types of allowed equipment, naturally, were limited to what he sold in his sporting goods stores. Ironically, his marketing schemes, along with his aggressive monopolistic practices of subsuming most upstart, rival leagues, were markedly un-democratic and ultimately unfriendly to the middle class, economically speaking. Stephen Hardy looks at the development of the sporting goods industry in the late nineteenth/early twentieth centuries as a major factor in the "leisure revolution" that, in his words, "turned informal pastimes into commodities" by assuming power over different leisure industries. Hardy wonders to what degree sport can really be considered leisure if an industry of providers chooses the physical equipment, controls the physical space, and governs the use of the services (73).

7. If anything, the fictional narrative of baseball's origins have only strengthened throughout the years. The Baseball Hall of Fame in Doubleday's hometown of Cooperstown makes this fabricated history a very prominent part of its marketing campaign. The narrative of America's development of baseball is exemplified in Cooperstown's current traveling museum exhibit, "Baseball as America."

8. Richard Butsch argues that while Olmstead's ideas for creating natural parks as leisure spaces were, in *theory,* designed to act this way, in *practice* they fell victim to limited success. Butsch sees the issue of control as one of the major problems with the park movement; upper class financiers or middle class citizens of the progressive era sought to "co-opt space for their own leisure or control the recreations of the working class" but soon discovered that the working class's desire to enjoy free time in their own fashion provided too much resistance (13).

9. Spalding also embarked upon several crusades to colonize other nations with baseball; for several years, he formed an all-star team that traveled

to the Pacific Islands, to South America, to Europe, and to Asia, playing exhibition games and creating opportunities for Spalding to talk about the "American" game of baseball.

10. Who often dined with Grantland Rice at Ring Lardner's home.

11. This scene has been mentioned critically in only a few places. Bruccoli merely says that it was deleted "first, to remove Gatsby's weakness and, second, to make Tom's defeat of Gatsby more convincing" (18); Lauricella argues in an analytical note that Fitzgerald "rewrote the entire chapter without the intrusive (in this case) baseball material to obviate any deflection of course or depression of intensity" (94); Johnson agrees with Lauricella by saying that baseball works in the novel "on a metaphorical level that might have been diffused if an important scene at the Polo Grounds used baseball as scenery instead of symbol" (38). The text of the passage itself, as well as the implication of its excision in light of the cultural significance of baseball, has not been analyzed.

12. From this point on, quotations contained in the manuscript, whether from the alternate scenes or from the scenes which were eventually published, will be noted in the parenthetical citation with "Manuscript"; Those cited as *Gatsby* come from the published edition.

13. For a historical recounting of the events surrounding the Black Sox scandal of 1919, see Eliot Asinof's *Eight Men Out*. See also Lauricella for a critical argument concerning faith, religion, and innocence as portrayed in this episode in the novel.

14. That this observation is made by Nick Carraway is ironic considering the fact that Nick, who although at times entertains a fondness for growing middle-class American progress, more often aligns himself with the tradition and breeding of privileged characters such as Tom (see Mallios 382–383, Michaels 41).

15. For a comprehensive discussion of Fitzgerald's treatment of Jewishness in *The Great Gatsby* as well as in other novels and stories, see Alan Margolies's "The Maturing of F. Scott Fitzgerald."

NOTES TO THE CODA

1. Grandnephew of the famous American author.

Bibliography

Adelman, Melvin. *A Sporting Time: New York City and the Rise of Modern Athletics, 1820–1870.* Urbana: U of Illinois P, 1986.

Adorno, Theodor and Max Horkheimer. "The Culture Industry: Enlightenment as Mass Deception." *Dialectic of Enlightenment.* Trans. John Cumming. New York: Continuum, 1995.

Bederman, Gail. *Manliness and Civilization: A Cultural History of Gender and Race in the United States, 1880–1917.* Chicago: U of Chicago P, 1995.

Bender, Bert. "'His Mind Aglow': The Biological Undercurrent in Fitzgerald's *Gatsby* and other works." *Journal of American Studies* 32.3: 399–420.

Berman, Ronald. *Fitzgerald, Hemingway, and the Twenties.* Tuscaloosa: U of Alabama P, 2001.

Bernstein, Mark F. *Football: The Ivy League Origins of an American Obsession.* Philadelphia: U of Philadelphia P, 2001.

Bourdieu, Pierre. *Algeria 1960: The Disenchantment of the World, the Sense of Honour, the Kabyle House or the World Reversed.* Trans. Richard Nice. Cambridge: Cambridge UP.

Boorstin, Daniel. *The Image: A Guide to Pseudo-Events in America.* New York: Harper and Row, 1964.

Brooks, David. "The Organization Kid." *Atlantic Monthly,* April 2001. March 29, 2004. <http://www.theatlantic.com/issues/2001/04/brooks-p1.htm>.

Brown, Bill. *The Material Unconscious: American Amusement, Stephen Crane, and the Economies of Play.* Cambridge, MA: Harvard UP, 1996.

Bruccoli, Matthew J. *Apparatus for The Great Gatsby.* Columbia: U of South Carolina P, 1974.

Bryant, Jennings and Steven Rockwell. "'Buzzer Beaters' and 'Barn Burners': The Effects on Enjoyment of Watching the Game Go 'Down to the Wire.'" *Journal of Sport and Social Issue.* 18.4 (1994): 326–340.

Bryer, Jackson R., ed. *New Essays on F. Scott Fitzgerald's Neglected Stories.* Columbia: U of Missouri P, 1996.

Burk, Robert. *Never Just a Game: Players, Owners, and American Baseball to 1920.* Chapel Hill: U of North Carolina P, 1994.

Bush, George H.W. "Inaugural Address." Washington, DC. 20 Jan., 1991. Ed. *The American Presidency Project.* 17 Dec., 2004. <http://www.americanpresidency. org>.

———. "Remarks Congratulating the Super Bowl Champion San Francisco 49ers." Washington, DC. 27 Feb. 1990. Ed. *The American Presidency Project.* 1 March 2005. <http://www.americanpresidency.org>.

Butler, J.A. "Community Baseball." *The Athletic Journal.* Jan., 1925. 5 (8):23–5.

Butsch, Richard. "Leisure and Hegemony in America." *For Fun and Profit.* Ed. Richard Butsch. Philadelphia: Temple UP, 1990.

Cady, Edwin H. *The Big Game: College Sports and American Life.* Knoxville: U of Tennessee P, 1978.

Callahan, John F. *The Illusions of a Nation: Myth and History in the Novels of F. Scott Fitzgerald.* Urbana: U of Illinois P, 1972.

Camp, Walter. *The Book of Foot-ball.* New York: The Century, 1910.

———. "College Football." *Outing,* 17 (1891); 385–390.

Chadwick, Henry. [Untitled.] *Ball Players' Chronicle* 26 Sept., 1867.

Cronin, Mike. *Sport and Nationalism in Ireland.* Portland, OR: Four Courts, 1999.

Daniel, Anne Margaret. "'Blue as the Sky, Gentlemen': Fitzgerald's Princeton through *The Prince.*" *F. Scott Fitzgerald in the Twenty-First Century.* Ed. Jackson R. Bryer, Ruth Prigozy, and Milton R. Stern. Tuscaloosa: U of Alabama P, 2003.

Davies, John. "It's Baker! Going For Another Touchdown!" *Esquire* 66.3 (1966): 132–35, 171–76.

Douglas, Ann. *Terrible Honesty: Mongrel Manhattan in the 1920s.* New York: Farrar, Straus, and Giroux, 1995.

Dugdale, Timothy. "The Fan and (Auto)Biography: Writing the Self in the Stars." *Journal of Mundane Behavior.* 1.2 (2000). 3 Dec. 2004. <http://www.mundanebehavior.org/issues/v1n2/dugdale.htm>.

Dunning, Eric. "The Figurational Approach to Leisure and Sport." *Leisure for Leisure.* Ed. Chris Rojek. New York: Routledge, 1989. 36–52.

Eble, Kenneth. *F. Scott Fitzgerald.* New York: Twayne, 1963.

Fimrite, Ron. "A Flame that Burned Too Brightly." *Sports Illustrated* March 18, 1991. 79–90.

Fitzgerald, F. Scott. "Author's House." *Esquire* 6 (July 1936): 40, 108.

———. "The Bowl." *The Saturday Evening Post* 100. (21 January 1928). 6–7, 93–94, 97, 100.

———. "The Crack-Up." *The Crack-Up, with Other Uncollected Pieces.* 5th edition. Ed. Edmund Wilson. New York: New Directions, 1993. 69–84.

———. *The Great Gatsby.* New York: Simon and Schuster, 1995.

———. *The Great Gatsby: A Fascimile of the Manuscript.* Ed. Matthew J. Bruccoli. Washington: Microcard Editions, 1973.

———. *Letters of F. Scott Fitzgerald.* Ed. Andrew Turnbull. New York: Scribner's, 1963.

———. *A Life in Letters.* Ed. Matthew J. Bruccoli. New York: Touchstone, 1994.

———. "'Send Me In, Coach.'" *Esquire's Second Sports Reader.* Ed. Arnold Gingrich. New York: Barnes, 1946. 34–44.

———. "Princeton." *Afternoon of an Author, a Selection of Uncollected Stories and Essays.* Ed. Arthur Mizener. New York: Scribner's, 1957. 93–103.

———. "Reade, Substitute Right Half." *The Apprentice Fiction of F. Scott Fitzgerald, 1909–1917.* Ed. John R. Kuehl. New Brunswick, NJ: Rutgers UP, 1965. 28–33.

———. "Ring." *The Crack-Up, with Other Uncollected Pieces.* 5th edition. Ed. Edmund Wilson. New York: New Directions, 1993. 13–22.

———. *This Side of Paradise.* Ed. James L. West III. New York: Cambridge UP, 1995.

———. "Sleeping and Waking." *The Crack-Up, with Other Uncollected Pieces.* 5th edition. Ed. Edmund Wilson. New York: New Directions, 1993. 65–6.

Folsom, Ed. *Walt Whitman's Native Representations.* New York: Cambridge UP, 1994.

"Freshman Handbook." Class of 1917. Seely G. Mudd Manuscript Library, Princeton University Library. Published with permission of Princeton University Library.

Fussell, Paul. *Class: A Guide Through the American Status System.* New York: Summit Books, 1983.

Gardner, Ralph D. "Alger Heroes, the Merriwells, et al!" *The Princeton University Library Chronicle* 30.2 (Winter 1969): 103–9.

Gipe, George. *The Great American Sports Book.* Garden City, NY: Doubleday, 1978.

Goffman, Erving. *The Presentation of Self in Everyday Life.* Garden City, NY: Doubleday, 1959.

Golenbock, Peter. *Wrigleyville: A Magical History Tour of the Chicago Cubs.* New York: St. Martin's, 1996.

Gorn, Elliot. "Spectator Sports." *The Reader's Companion to American History.* Houghton Mifflin. 22 July 2004. <http://college.hmco.com/history/ readerscomp/rcah/html/ah_081100_spectatorspo.htm>.

Grange, Red. *The Red Grange Story: An Autobiography.* Urbana: U of Illinois P, 1993.

Hardin, Mary Myers and Brent Hardin. "The 'Supercrip' in Sport Media: Wheelchair Athletes Discuss Hegemony's Disabled Hero." *Sociology of Sport Online.* 7.1 (2004). 17 Dec., 2004. <http://physed.otago.ac.nz/sosol/v7i1/v7i1_1.html>.

Hardy, Stephen. "'Adopted By All the Leading Clubs': Sporting Goods and the Shaping of Leisure, 1800–1900." *For Fun and Profit.* Ed. Richard Butsch. Philadelphia: Temple UP, 1990.

Henderson, Robert W. *Ball, Bat and Bishop: The Origin of Ball Games.* Urbana: U of Illinois P, 2001.

Herr, Cheryl. *Joyce's Anatomy of Culture.* Urbana: U of Illinois P, 1986.

Higgins, John A. *F. Scott Fitzgerald: A Study of the Stories.* New York: St. John's UP, 1971.

Higham, John. *Strangers in the Land.* New Brunswick, NJ: Rutgers UP, 1981.

Higham, John. *The Origins of Modern Consciousness.* Detroit: Wayne State UP, 1965.

Hynd, Noel. *The Giants of the Polo Grounds: The Glorious Times of Baseball's New York Giants.* New York: Doubleday, 1988.

Inabinett, Mark. *Grantland Rice and His Heroes : The Sportswriter as Mythmaker in the 1920s.* Knoxville: U of Tennessee P, 1994.

James, Pearl. "History and Masculinity in F. Scott Fitzgerald's this Side of Paradise." *Modern Fiction Studies* 51.1 (2005). 1–33.

Johnson, Larry. NBA Finals Pre-game Interview. 24 June 1999.

Johnson, Robert Jr. "Fitzgerald's Use of Baseball in *The Great Gatsby.*" *The F. Scott Fitzgerald Review* 1 (2002). 3–44.

Kalra, Paul. *The American Class System: Divide and Rule.* Pleasant Hill, CA: Antenna, 1995.

Kirsch, George B. *The Creation of American Team Sports.* Urbana: U of Illinois P, 1989.

Klein, Alan M. *Sugarball: The American Game, the Dominican Dream.* New Haven, CT: Yale UP, 1991.

Laberge, Suzanne. "Toward an Integration of Gender into Bourdieu's Concept of Cultural Capital." *Sociology of Sport* 12.2: 132–146.

Landis, Kennesaw Mountain. "Judge Landis Endorses Junior Baseball." *The Athletic Journal.* Nov, 1924. 18:469.

Lauricella, John A. "The Black Sox Signature Baseball in *The Great Gatsby.*" *Aethlon* 10.1 (Fall 1992): 83–98.

Leitch, Alexander. "The Eating Clubs." *A Princeton Companion.* Princeton, NJ: Princeton UP, 1978. 3 April 2004. <http://etc.princeton.edu/CampusWWW/Companion/eating_clubs.html>.

Lessa, Richard. "'Our Nervous, Sporadic Games': Sports in *The Great Gatsby.*" *Arete: The Journal of Sport Literature.* 1.2 (Spring 1984): 69–79.

Levine, Peter. *A.G. Spalding and the Rise of Baseball: The Promise of American Sport.* New York: Oxford UP, 1985.

Lisle, Ben. "Commodifying Leisure: The Business of Baseball in the Guilded Age." December 2000. University of Virginia American Studies. 2 March 2004. <http://xroads.virginia.edu/~HYPER/INCORP/baseball/contents.html>.

Magazine Clipping, *The Sporting News.* John D. Davies Collection of Hobey Baker. Box 2, Princeton University Library. Seely G. Mudd Manuscript Library. Published with permission of Princeton University Library.

Mallios, Peter. "Undiscovering the Country: Conrad, Fitzgerald, and Meta-National Form." *Modern Fiction Studies* 47.2 (2001): 356–390.

Mangum, Bryant. "The Short Stories of F. Scott Fitzgerald." *The Cambridge Companion to F. Scott Fitzgerald.* Ed. Ruth Prigozy. New York: Cambridge UP, 2002. 57–78.

Margolies, Alan. "The Maturing of F. Scott Fitzgerald." *Twentieth Century Literature* 43.1 (Spring 1997): 75–93.

McGraw, John J. "Baseball Has Changed Some in Thirty Years, Says John J. McGraw." *The Literary Digest* 62 (10 May, 1919): 96.

Melville, Tom. *Early Baseball and the Rise of the National League.* Jefferson, NC: McFarland & Co., 2001.

Messenger, Christian K. *Sport and the Spirit of Play in American Fiction: Hawthorne to Faulkner.* New York: Columbia UP, 1981.

Michaels, Walter Benn. *Our America: Nativism, Modernism, and Pluralism.* Durham, NC: Duke UP, 1995.

Michener, James. *Sports in America.* New York: Random House, 1976.

Newcombe, Jack. *The Best of the Athletic Boys: The White Man's Impact on Jim Thorpe.* Garden City, NY: Doubleday, 1975.

Newspaper Clipping, *Brooklyn Daily Eagle.* John D. Davies Collection of Hobey Baker. Box 2, Seely G. Mudd Manuscript Library, Princeton University Library. Published with permission of Princeton University Library.

Neyer, Rob. "Why Do We Care So Much?" *ESPN.com.* 16 Oct. 2003. ESPN. 17 Oct. 2003. <http://sports.espn.go.com/mlb/playoffs2003/columns/story?columnist=neyer_rob&id=1640230>.

Notes, John D. Davies Collection of Hobey Baker. Box 3. Seely G. Mudd Manuscript Library, Princeton University Library. Published with permission of Princeton University Library.

Novak, Michael. *The Joy of Sports: End Zones, Bases, Baskets, Ball.* New York: Basic Books, 1976.

Oriard, Michael. *Reading Football: How the Popular Press Created an American Spectacle.* Chapel Hill: U of North Carolina P, 1993.

———. *Sporting with the Gods: The Rhetoric of Play and Game in American Culture.* New York: Cambridge UP, 1991.

Palmatier, Robert and Harold Ray. *Sports Talk: A Dictionary of Sports Metaphors.* Westport, CT: Greenwood, 1989.

Parrish, Michael E. *Anxious Decades: America in Prosperity and Depression, 1920–1941.* New York: Norton, 1992.

Perrin, Tom. *Football: A College History.* Jefferson, NC: Mcfarland & Company, 1987.

Powel, Harford Jr. *Walter Camp: The Father of American Football.* Boston: Little, 1926.

Princeton Eating Club Records Finding Aid. "History." Department of Rare Books and Special Collections, Princeton University Library. 7 April 2004. <http://libweb.princeton.edu/libraries/firestone/rbsc/finding_aids/eat-club.html>.

Real, Michael and Robert Mechikoff. "Deep Fan: Mythic Identification, Technology, and Advertising in Spectator Sports." *Journal of Sport Sociology* 9 (1993): 323–339.

Roosevelt, Theodore. "The Value of an Athletic Training." *Harper's Weekly* December 23, 1893: 1236.

Schechner, Richard. "What is Performance?" *Performance Studies: An Introduction.* New York: Routledge, 2002. 22–44.

Schickel, Richard. *Intimate Strangers: The Culture of Celebrity.* Chicago: Dee, 2000.

Seymour, Harold. "Baseball: Badge of Americanism." *Cooperstown Symposium on Baseball and the American Culture.* Ed. Alvin Hall, Jr. Westport, CT: Meckler, 1990. 1–22.

Sklar, Robert. *F. Scott Fitzgerald: The Last Laocoön.* New York: Oxford UP, 1967.

Smith, Brian. "So Long Sammy, We Hardly Knew You." *The Daily Vanguard.* 22 Feb., 2006. Portland State University. 25 Sept. 2006. <http://www.dailyvanguard.com/vnews/display.v?TARGET=printable&article_id=43fce6c18f4fe>

Solomon, Eric. "Jews and Baseball: A Cultural Love Story." *The Charisma of Sport and Race.* Ed. Gillis, Christina M. Berkeley: U of California-Berkeley P, 1996.

Sosa, Sammy and Marcos Bretón. *Sosa: An Autobiography.* New York: Warner, 2000.

Spalding, Albert G. *America's National Game.* New York: American Sports Publishing Company, 1911.

Standish, Burt L. *Frank Merriwell at Yale.* Philadelphia: McKay, 1903.

———. "Frank Merriwell Tested, or a Doubtful Honor." *Tip Top Weekly* 196 (Jan. 13, 1900).

———. "Frank Merriwell's Fun." *Tip Top Weekly* 281 (Aug. 31 1901).

Stark, Jayson. "Say it Ain't So." *ESPN.com.* 14 Oct. 2003. ESPN. 15 Oct. 2003. <http://sports.espn.go.com/mlb/playoffs2003/columns/story?columnist= stark_jayson&id=1638362>.

Sugden, John and Alan Tomlinson. "Theorizing Sport, Social Class and Status." *Handbook of Sports Studies.* Ed. Jay Coakley, and Eric Dunning, London: Sage, 2000.

Traubel, Horace. *With Walt Whitman in Camden.* Boston: Small, 1906.

Trilling, Lionel. "F. Scott Fitzgerald." Donaldson, Scott, ed. *Critical Essays on F. Scott Fitzgerald's* The Great Gatsby. Boston: Hall, 1984.

Tygiel, Jules. *Past Time: Baseball as History.* New York: Oxford UP, 2000.

[Untitled]. *The New York Clipper* 7 (July 2, 1859): 84.

[Untitled]. *The Spirit of the Times* 22 (July 16, 1870): 343.

Veblen, Thorstein. *The Theory of the Leisure Class.* Penguin Classics Edition. New York: Penguin, 1994.

Ward, Geoffrey C. *Baseball: An Illustrated History.* New York: Knopf, 1994.

Way, Brian. *F. Scott Fitzgerald and the Art of Social Fiction.* New York: St. Martin's, 1980.

Weber, Max. "Class, Status, Power." *From Max Weber: Essays in Sociology.* Trans. H. H. Gerth and C. Wright Mills. New York: Oxford UP, 1946.

White, Hayden. *The Content of the Form: Narrative Discourse and Historical Representation.* Baltimore: Johns Hopkins UP, 1987.

"White House Dream Team." *www.whitehousekids.gov.* 9 April 2004. The White House. 23 July 2004. <http://www.whitehouse.gov/kids/dreamteam/index. html>.

Zevenbergen, Robin, Allan Edwards, and James Skinner. "Junior Golf Club Culture: A Bourdieuian Analysis." *Sociology of Sport Online.* 5.1 (2002). 7 Apr., 2005. <http://physed.otago.ac.nz/sosol/v5i1/v5i1bordeau.html>.

Index